Southern cultures

Fall 2006
Published by the
University of North Carolina Press
for the
Center for the Study of the American South
at the University of North Carolina at Chapel Hill

Books

front porch

Aside from moonlight and magnolias, there can't be many things more stereotypically southern than frilly ornamental ironwork veiling the balconies around some timeless antebellum square. In truth, only a few places in the South are famous for such vistas — Charleston, New Orleans, and Mobile come immediately to mind — but these iconic cities are so famous as epitomes of antebellum charm that exotic features of their landscapes can somehow seem more typical of the region than reality itself. Lacy antique grillwork might be nonexistent in your county or mine, but if you do see one of those ornate filigrees framed around a live oak limb, preferably one laden with Spanish moss, you *know* you're in the South.

John Sledge and Sheila Hagler share a portrait of historic cast iron décor from Mobile, Alabama, taken from their new book, *An Ornament to the City: Old Mobile Ironwork* (Athens: University of Georgia Press, 2006). It's impossible to argue with their subject. With a moment's thought, we all know that the mansions and public buildings adorned by Mobile's iron tracery were monuments to the planters and cotton factors of antebellum elite. We also know who could and who could not enjoy the public parks with their gently splashing fountains. When all is said and done, however, these ugly realities inevitably fade. The lacy metal itself is just too beautiful, whether seen up close in delicate detail or admired from across the square. Soft and delicate in appearance, rigid and obdurate in the face of time, it's easy to see why ornamental iron became such a powerful symbol or a stereotype for the beauty and mystery we may want to believe about the South.

Stereotypes are powerful themes in southern culture. Whether framing the balconies of Mobile or a mental image of white robes and crinolines, stereotypes seem to be essential to our thinking about the place, and that's true whether we are southerners or not. If we didn't know that by instinct, Larry Griffin has taken the trouble to prove it to us in a careful exploration of southern opinion polls, especially the Southern Focus Polls conducted by the Odum Institute for Research in the Social Sciences at UNC-CH in the 1990s.

Griffin picks up on an idea first voiced by John Reed, retired UNC-CH sociologist and founder of *Southern Cultures*. What is it that makes people think of them-

left:

John Sledge and Sheila Hagler's "Lacy Charm in Old Mobile: The Historic Cast Iron of Alabama's First City" shows how Victorian Mobilians — and residents of the city years later — fell in love with cast iron's decorative possibilities. The Richards House (1860), Mobile, Alabama, photographed by Sheila Hagler.

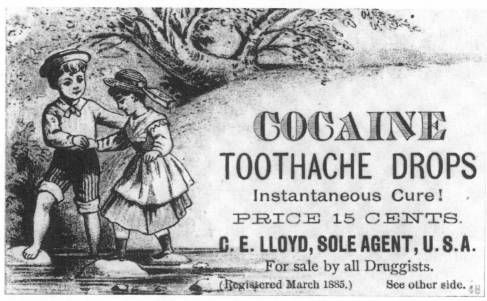

Michael M. Cohen looks at the interplay of race and drug use in the South in "Jim Crow's Drug War: Race, Coca Cola, and the Southern Origins of Drug Prohibition." Patent medicines used to promise cures for just about every ailment. Advertisement from Michael M. Cohen's collection.

selves as southerners? It isn't just birth, because some people become adopted southerners and some born Dixie-ites renounce the place. Nor is it residence, because some people who live in the South—white and black—don't think of themselves as southern. So what is it?

A key part of the answer, Griffin finds, depends on stereotypes. If you think the South is a warm and friendly place to live, for example, and you think of yourself as a warm and friendly person, and if you are born or live in the South, then you are much more likely to think of yourself as a southerner than someone who does not believe those things. It sounds simple when you put it that way, but it also confirms something profound. Regional identity is something intimate and powerful. It gets deep down into your personality and stays there, so that what kind of person you want to be and what kind of group identity you embrace become densely interwoven. Kind of like a twining tendril of ornamental ironwork, looping around your life in a filmy but unbreakable lattice.

So if stereotypes are so important, what's inside the stereotypes that govern southern identity? That gets more complicated. Any cheap-shot regional culture expert will tell you that the South is both friendly and hateful, languid and violent, over-sexed and cruelly repressed, and suffused with the religion of the Christian Right except when it's engulfed by the religion of the Civil Rights Movement. We'll vote dry as long as we can stagger to the polls, and our region of illiterates has produced America's finest writers. The list of contradictions goes on and on. With so much at stake, it's well that we examine our stereotypes with special care.

Let's take the war on drugs. We all know that the Bible Belt is especially stern on mind-altering substances, except for Grandpa's moonshine and Grandma's nerve tonic. The modern technology of narcotics has had a devastating impact on individuals, families, and communities all over the world, but different countries deal with the problem in different ways. Some regard addiction as an incurable accident, and treat the addict as someone who unfortunately needs to be medicated, much like an amputee who needs an artificial limb. In the United States, we treat the addict as a moral failure who ought to be reclaimed or even punished instead of coddled. Why the difference?

Michael Cohen addresses the answer in his article about the South's experience with cocaine. First praised as an antidote to morphine addiction among genteel neurasthenics, then relished as the secret behind Coca-Cola, cocaine became fearsome to southern whites when it crossed the color line. Ironically, late nineteenth-century white employers introduced cocaine to their black laborers to dull their pain and make them work harder. Not long afterwards, however, stories of cocaine-maddened Negroes filled the southern press and spiced the image of the "black beast rapist" that inspired lynch mobs and Jim Crow legislation alike. The stereotype spread northward with the Great Migration, and legislative bodies nationwide were soon passing laws aimed at a racially-tinged drug threat. If anything, the image of the drug-crazed black criminal is even stronger now than it was a century ago, when Asa Candler prudently switched ingredients in "the real thing." So which stereotype is the truest? The addicted aristocrat Mrs. Henry Lafayette Dubose from Harper Lee's *To Kill a Mockingbird*, or Nancy Manigo, the murdering black "dope fiend whore" in William Faulkner's *Requiem for a Nun*? Southern literature has gotten a lot of mileage out of both, but lots of us would agree that both fall a bit short of typical, to say the least.

At roughly the same time that millions of Americans began to love Coke and fear cocaine, the state of Tennessee was cultivating another image-based product. The Civil War had been deeply divisive in Tennessee, with many white Tennesseans opposing secession and cooperating with Union invaders. By 1900, the generation who had fought the war was facing old age. Their children longed to give the old gentlemen the respect they thought proper and also to leave an impression in historical memory in which the divisions and disorders of the real War were swept away by tales of unanimous valor.

This was the environment that raised a thousand shafts across the South's courthouse lawns. It also supported a special Tennessee cult around Sam Davis, a young Confederate spy hanged by Union forces near the town of Pulaski in

1863. In another look at southern stereotypes, Edward John Harcourt shows us that there was nothing really extraordinary about Sam Davis, for he was one of many Tennesseans hanged for espionage by Civil War armies on both sides. But Sam Davis's historical image was something else, carefully crafted by a Confederate veteran named Sumner Cunningham who overcame his own shady wartime record with a postwar career as a fulsome professional memorialist of the Lost Cause. In Cunningham's capable hands, Sam Davis became the Confederate Nathan Hale, a model for flawless manhood and selfless valor, whose very defeat somehow became the source of the white South's enduring strength.

The South has its counter-stereotypes as well. Filmmaker Kevin Willmott has played with quite a few of these in his recent movie *C.S.A.: The Confederate States of America*. A parody of TV documentaries, *C.S.A.* poses as a report on life in a modern America in which the South has won the Civil War. The central theme, of course, is that slavery would still be the foundation of American civilization, with all of modern technology harnessed for the exploitation of black Americans. To make this point, Willmott carries the rewriting of history a step further and imagines that southern victory would have meant Confederate annexation of the entire United States instead of simple southern independence. The effect is to create a biting critique of America itself instead of our isolated part of it—a reconsideration of the old gibe attributed to Malcolm X that "the South begins at the Canadian border." Linkages to current events start right away in the movie's trailer, in which blue Union states in a U.S. map all change colors until the entire country is one big Red State, from Hawaii to Maine. Literary critic Trudier Harris

Edward John Harcourt examines Tennessee's tributes to Confederate spy Sam Davis in "The Boys Will Have to Fight the Battles without Me." A view of wartime Nashville from the steps of the state capitol, courtesy of the Collections of the Library of Congress.

thinks Willmot has carried the gag too far, and shares her reasons in a probing review of *C.S.A.*

Which stereotype represents the "real" South—the violent addict, the noble soldier, the slavetrading hellhole? Real life has produced plentiful examples of each, but few would still argue that any of these images encompasses the whole of southern life. In our "Not Forgotten" section, however, Michael Parker shares a southern memory that draws a bit on old stereotypes but breaks new ground. It's a story from the early days of integration in Clinton, North Carolina, when the author found himself the only white boy in the brass section of his high school marching band. Intoxicated by the black music of the 1970s, he and his fellow horn players were thrilled by the chance to electrify the halftime crowd with their rendition of Isaac Hayes's unforgettable theme from *Shaft*. As a movie, *Shaft* drew on some stereotypes of its own, with a lineage of romantic black bad men stretching back to Railroad Bill and Stagolee, if not further. Hayes's score matched the image perfectly—cool, smooth, powerful, sexy, irresistible, incomparably baaaaaad. . . The kids at Clinton—black and white, fat and thin, male and female—were not only sick of themselves for all the usual teenage reasons, but they were undoubtedly sick of racial tension too. They wanted a piece of the super-cool black bad man image for themselves so bad they couldn't stand themselves all over again.

Well, it would spoil a good story if everything turned out the way you'd expect, but Parker tells it best. The picture that stayed with me the longest, however, was the four horn players bonding together, linked by their common love of *"Shaft"* and what it represented and their common hatred of their "fascist" band leader. That's a southern stereotype we should all be able to relate to. If that's in the social psychology of southern identity, I think we need a lot more of it.

HARRY L. WATSON, *Coeditor*

The American South and the Self

by Larry J. Griffin

Each region of the United States has a particular identity hewn from history and culture. Yet none is as distinctive as the American South and none has been imbued with such historical weight in the nation's making or afforded such metaphorical significance in its collective memory and mythological self-understandings. Southern icon Robert E. Lee, frontispiece photograph from Henry Alexander White's Robert E. Lee and the Southern Confederacy, 1807–1870, *published by G. P. Putnam's Sons in 1897.*

ach region of the United States has a particular identity hewn from history and culture. Yet none is as distinctive as the American South, and none has been imbued with such historical weight in the nation's making or afforded such metaphorical significance in its collective memory and mythological self-understandings. For centuries New England was understood as the genesis and crystallization of "American civilization" and the endlessly unfolding, ever renewing West as the embodiment of America's promise. The South, however, was America's opposite, its negative image, its evil twin—"an alien member of the national family," in literary critic Fred Hobson's apt phrase. "The South"—more accurately, the white South—thus was in word and deed "exceptional" among places in America: exceptional in its fierce commitment to slavery, in its failed experiment with secession and nationhood, in its military defeat and occupation by a conquering power, in its poverty, cultural backwardness, and religiosity, and in its pervasive, prolonged resistance to racial justice.

This exceptionalism, as much in identity as in practice, historically has been so profound as to provoke repeated changes in the nation's laws governing citizenship rights. As Sanford Levinson, a professor of constitutional law at the University of Texas, argues, "The issues presented by the South, as a distinctive region [of the United States], have, since the founding of our nation, presented the most exquisite difficulties in terms of establishing a truly coherent national identity." In establishing this unified national identity, the region has served as, in historian Carl Degler's terms, America's indispensable "antithesis," the country's "other," a cathartic, dialectical counterpoint always shadowing America's self-idealizations; consequently, the South has been the motive and the "stage" for redemptive collective action in what southern writer J. Bill Berry cites as "the nation's major moral drama."[1]

Definitions of a region and its culture as "exceptional"—that is, as significantly distinct from, seemingly at times even antithetical to, other regions and cultures—inevitably also identify in particular ways its folk. Just as the history of the South is contradictory and contested, so, too, is the identity of southerners. Two very different but interdependent processes are crucial here: one of collective definition of the region and the other of the social psychology of regional identification. On the question of collective definition, what it means to be a southerner is a complex and historically shifting consequence of imposition of laws, images, stereotypes, and the like by powerful forces in the public arena (such as military victors, political majorities, the federal government, and the media), negotiation of meaning among southerners and between southerners and others, and cultural appropriation, whereby a debased label associated with "southernness," such as "redneck" or "hillbilly," is transmuted from a mark of stigma to one of pride by those who are so labeled. On the question of the social psychology of regional-

"The South" — the white South — was in word and deed "exceptional" among places in America: exceptional in its fierce commitment to slavery, in its failed experiment with secession and nationhood, in its military defeat and occupation by a conquering power, in its poverty, cultural backwardness, and religiosity, and in its pervasive, prolonged resistance to racial justice. Photograph courtesy of Wilson Library's Southern Historical Collection at the University of North Carolina at Chapel Hill.

ism, why individuals identify themselves as "southerners"—whatever the collective meaning of the identity—on the other hand, is a function of choices they make—choices, however, constrained by biography, perception of the region and its inhabitants, and social interactions, with some southerners arguably having greater latitude in their self-definitions than others.[2]

Many southerners are marked, as are members of racial and ethnic groups, by ascriptive or quasi-ascriptive characteristics—accents in particular—and so may be defined, morally as well as cognitively, by others as "southern" regardless of their own initial self-definitions. Given the imposed meaning of "southerner," nonsoutherners are also apt to interact with people they perceive to be southern, due to their accents or where they are from, as if they *were* "southerners"—or at least their idea of "southern"—thus reproducing regional stereotypes and collective definitions. Southerners who experience this treatment might themselves then internalize the label (if not necessarily its collateral meanings), understand that others "like them" are similarly treated, and come to think of themselves as "southern." One person in sociologist John Shelton Reed's 1971 study of the regional social psychology of North Carolinians put it this way when asked why she identified as a southerner: "Most everyone around here feels they are Southerners, and so I guess I do, too."[3]

Geography may not be destiny, but neither is identification with the region or

One participant in Reed's 1971 study said of the South: "I like the slow pace. Also the friendliness."
Photograph courtesy of Wilson Library's Southern Historical Collection at the University of North
Carolina at Chapel Hill.

as a southerner a matter of unadulterated individual choice for many. If southern culture is the only one southerners have experienced, or if it at least was their formative one, they may have difficulty in not using the region as a source of personal identity simply because that is where they are from and that is what they know of themselves in regional terms. Several of Reed's 1971 interviewees expressed this point with eloquent simplicity: "The reason I feel that way is that's all I know. I don't know any different than the South." And, "I guess it's because I've always been told—brought up that way, I guess." Survey data from the 1991–2001 Southern Focus Polls (SFP) indicate that more than 87 percent of Dixie's residents with moderate or strong regional accents and 93 percent of those who have always lived in the South—"ascribed southerners," in Reed's terminology—understand themselves to be southerners. Conversely, the minority of southerners with sustained experience of different cultures, such as adult transplants into the region, for example, or those with ready access to potentially powerful competing social identities defined by ethnicity, religion, or race—Hispanics, Asians, Catholics, and Jews, most obviously—are less likely to identify themselves as southerners, especially if they find its collective or stereotyped definitions unpleasant.[4]

Still, southerners are free in principle both to select which images of the South they use for reference purposes and to define themselves or not in terms of their region, whatever others may attribute to or about them. This is most clearly observed when we look at Reed's categories of "lapsed southerners," those life-long southerners who, for reasons of residence or accent, ascriptively "ought" to identify as southerners but do not, and their counterparts in the region, "assimilated nonsoutherners," the in-migrants who ascriptively "ought not" to do so but nonetheless understand themselves in regional terms. Lapsed southerners presumably find the collective definition of "southerner" repellent or simply inconsistent with who they understand themselves to be and reject it as a meaningful self-descriptor. One lapsed southerner in Reed's study of North Carolinians was quite clear about why he refused to think of himself as a southerner: "I'm not the typical Southerner—too liberal." He, clearly, stereotyped the South as conservative, an act in itself a form of constrained choice, and then compared himself to this stereotype. Finding that he did not "fit" this regional image, he chose not to be a southerner. Other lapsed southerners rejected the sectional connotations of "southerner," reporting that they "don't section themselves" and thus were "just all-American." According to the SFP results, 21 percent of those in the region who refuse to define themselves as southerners have lived in the region their entire lives: they're lapsed southerners. Assimilated nonsoutherners—22 percent of self-proclaimed southerners are migrants to the region, and 18 percent have no discernable southern accent—on the other hand, seem to find the region attractive for all sorts of reasons and use these perceptions to shift psychologically from the identity of "nonsoutherner" to the identity of "southerner." "Southerners are sincere and lovable," claimed one in-migrant in Reed's 1971 study. "We feel much more at home here." And, from another transplant who asserted her southernness, "I like the slow pace. Also the friendliness."[5]

Such folks seem to enjoy a fair amount of latitude about their choice of identities and may think of themselves as "southern" for reasons quite different from those for whom identity is ascriptively imposed or geographically and experientially limited. Yet even "ascribed" southerners may view their regional identity as salient because they may believe it both differentiates them from the mass of Americans and permits them membership in a largely imagined community of ancestral and honorific significance. To do this, though, they would have to ignore or discount the region's negative stereotypes: such southerners would need to believe the South distinctive, otherwise they could not use the region to set themselves apart from other Americans, but distinctive in a positive way. This form of "symbolic southernness"—a choice likely more prevalent now than in earlier decades due to the increasing Americanization of Dixie since the 1960s and 1970s, particularly with respect to race and politics—parallels the resurgence of symbolic ethnic sentiment among assimilated second- and third-generation white ethnics. Reed, in fact, has tackled the thorny issue of southern identity through the lens of the white ethnic experience in America.[6]

Despite white persecution and exclusion of African Americans throughout most of the South's history, black and white southerners express very similar levels of regional identity and judge the region in broadly similar ways, making suspect any statement about Dixie as a "whites-only" culture today. Photograph by Marion Post Walcott, 1939, courtesy of the Collections of the Library of Congress.

We know, then, that southerners do indeed make choices—some expected, some counterintuitive—about their regional identities. What we do not have much concrete information on, beyond Reed's interviews in 1971 with North Carolinians, is *why* they do so. Reed, who has thought more productively about this question than anyone, claims, against a purely ascriptive understanding, that "a regional group enlists the *identification* of its members. . . . [because] it serves them as a reference group to which they belong and is not just a [geographical] classification that happens to include them." From that premise, he argues that though residential and family history largely produce and validate a regional identity—much as national ancestry does in ethnic identity—the "social psychology of sectionalism" matters as well. To Reed, this peculiar mindset stems for white southerners (his focus) from a common history of sectional conflict with the North over slavery and, by the mid-twentieth century, of opposition to idealized American racial practices. Sectional conflict, in turn, produced both a largely defensive regional solidarity among southern whites and a stereotyped, "exceptional" white South easily accessed by them as a cultural category and reference group which, in turn, molded perceptions of in-group similarity/out-group dissimilarity. Spurred by this history and buttressed by the results of his 1971 survey of North Carolinians, Reed speculates, in particular, that folks will more likely think of themselves as southerners if they have a consciousness of the South as distinctive, perceive it in stereotypically positive ways (and spurn negative stereotypes), and identify with and believe themselves similar to others in the region and dissimilar from regional outsiders.[7]

Reed's major empirical work on these and similar issues, *Southerners*, analyzes the regional consciousness, stereotypes, grievances, and the like of whites in North Carolina in 1971 who identified themselves as southern, offering, along the way, insightful anecdotes from respondents about why they claimed or rejected a southern identity. But to the detriment of South-watchers everywhere, he has never found the time to explore fully the empirical implications of his ideas with more recent and geographically inclusive information. I do so with the six Southern Focus Polls containing questions that directly bear on and were motivated by Reed's theory of regional identification. Four of the polls surveyed both southerners (defined as inhabitants of the former Confederate states plus Kentucky and Oklahoma) and nonsoutherners (residents of other states), permitting regional comparisons: Fall 1992, Fall 1993, Fall 1995, Spring 1999. Two are limited to southerners: Fall 1991 (which also excludes Oklahoma) and Spring 1992. Although southerners were always over-sampled relative to their proportions in the

Even if the jury is still out on what nonsoutherners really believe about the South, it is clear, as Reed no doubt suspected, that southerners throughout the entire region bracingly affirm their region, especially so in contrast to northerners. The 20th Annual Museum of Appalachia's Tennessee Fall Homecoming, courtesy of Tennessee Tourist Development.

nation's population to insure a large statistical representation in the survey, and African Americans were occasionally over-sampled for the same reason, the SFP (save for the Fall 1991 survey) is broadly representative of the populations of the South and the nation.[8]

The questions I use and the Poll results are as follows below. (N refers to the number of respondents who provided valid answers):

Identification as a southerner (all Polls, 1991–2001): "Do you consider yourself a southerner, or not?" This question was asked only of those in the South.

	No	Yes	N
All southerners	26%	74%	17,186
Black southerners	23%	78%	2,936
White southerners	25%	75%	13,057

Perception of the distinctiveness of the South (Fall 1991, Spring 1992, Fall 1993): "Do you think that the South today has a lot of qualities that make it special and different from the rest of the United States, or is the South pretty much like any other part of the United States?"

	Like any other part of the U.S.	Special and different	N
All southerners	31%	69%	2,694
Black southerners	50%	50%	422
White southerners	27%	73%	2,138
Nonsoutherners	34%	66%	375

Perception that the South is the best region in which to live (Fall 1991, Spring 1992, Fall 1993): "Do you think that, all things considered, the South is the best region in the United States to live in, or do you think other parts of the country are as good or better?"

	Not best/ not better	Best region	N
All southerners	45%	55%	2,406
Black southerners	49%	52%	371
White southerners	44%	56%	1,922
Nonsoutherners	83%	17%	240

Holding positive stereotypes of southerners (Fall 1991, Spring 1992, Fall 1993, Fall 1995) is assessed with questions which asked, generally, whether the people in the region (as compared to those in other regions) were characterized as courteous, religious, friendly, conservative, etc.[9]

	% of Positive Stereotypes Held				
	Very few (0–39%)	Some (40–59%)	Many (60–79%)	Almost all/All (80–100%)	N
All southerners	17%	26%	29%	28%	2,715
Black southerners	19%	31%	25%	25%	460
White southerners	16%	25%	31%	29%	2,121
Nonsoutherners	36%	23%	34%	7%	453

Negative stereotypical views of southerners (Fall 1993): Believing that southerners, more than other Americans, are not hardworking, not intelligent, and violent.

	# of Negative Stereotypes Held				
	0	1	2	3	N
All southerners	59%	27%	10%	5%	705
Black southerners	57%	32%	6%	5%	79
White southerners	59%	26%	11%	4%	581
Nonsoutherners	61%	24%	12%	3%	316

Eighty-eight percent of African Americans and 91 percent of whites who believe the South is the best region in the country claim a southern identity. Visitors to Travellers Rest in Nashville, Tennessee, courtesy of Tennessee Tourist Development.

Regional consciousness (Spring 1992, Fall 1992): "How much thought would you say you have given to the South and to southerners before today?" Asked only of southerners.

	Almost none	Only a little	Some	Quite a bit	N
All southerners	17%	19%	26%	38%	1,548
Black southerners	24%	15%	27%	33%	190
White southerners	15%	20%	26%	39%	1,279

Interest in the success of other southerners (Spring 1992, Fall 1992): "How much interest would you say you have in how southerners as a whole are getting along in this country?" Asked only of southerners.

	Not much	Some	A great deal	N
All southerners	22%	38%	40%	1,504
Black southerners	20%	37%	44%	183
White southerners	21%	39%	40%	1,247

Closeness to other southerners (Spring 1992, Fall 1992, Fall 1999): "Some people in the South feel they have a lot in common with other southerners, but others we talk to don't feel this way. Would you say you feel pretty close to southerners in general, or that you don't feel much closer to them than you do to other people?" Asked only of southerners.

	Not close/Not closer	Close	N
All southerners	54%	46%	2,320
Black southerners	61%	39%	280
White southerners	52%	48%	1,892

Three patterns in the data are worthy of emphasis. First, a majority or near-majority of all southerners have a consciousness of, and think about, their region as a distinctive place in the American landscape, see it in quite positive ways (20 percent hold all of the positive stereotypes, and only 9 percent believe none of them) while also generally rejecting negative stereotypes (59 percent shun all negative stereotypes), and identify with other southerners, feeling close to them and expressing interest in what happens to them. Second, although African Americans are a bit less likely to view the region and its inhabitants positively, racial differences among southerners are generally small. The sole important exception to this generalization is that African Americans—perhaps unsurprisingly, given that race relations in the 1990s were strained throughout the entire country—are much less likely to perceive the region as exceptional. Despite white persecution and exclusion of African Americans throughout most of the South's history, black and white southerners thus express very similar levels of regional identity and judge the region in broadly similar ways, making suspect any statement about Dixie as a "whites-only" culture today. Third, southerners and nonsoutherners, even in the 1990s, when the SFPS were fielded, do not always share the same perceptions about the region. Northerners, like white southerners, acknowledge southern exceptionalism, but because they are far less likely than either black or white southerners to assert the region's superiority or to view it in stereotypically positive ways, they may not necessarily think this exceptionalism a good thing. (Only 4 percent hold all positive stereotypes.)[10]

How northerners perceive the South and southerners is difficult to gauge accurately, even in recent years. If the responses to questions in the SFP about negative regional stereotypes are to be believed, nonsoutherners are no more accepting of

Ninety percent or so of both blacks and whites who feel close to other southerners claim a southern identity. For these folks, whatever their race, it is almost impossible not to assert their southernness. Post-World War II sorority women at the University of North Carolina at Chapel Hill, courtesy of the North Carolina Collection in Wilson Library at the University of North Carolina at Chapel Hill.

them than are southerners. But should we believe these responses? Yankees' ostensibly unprejudiced views could reflect not true sentiment but what social scientists call "social desirability," a wish merely to avoid offending interviewers—many of whom spoke with a southern accent and were known to be affiliated with the University of North Carolina—or, more darkly, a desire to mask their own regional bigotry by saying little to suggest that they thought southerners loutish or an active danger to others. Data from other nationally representative surveys suggest that nonsoutherners' views are somewhat derogatory. Northerners in the 1990 General Social Survey (GSS), for example, more frequently asserted than did those south of the Mason-Dixon line that "white southerners" (the referent in the GSS stereotype questions) were significantly more likely to live off welfare rather than be self-supporting and to be more violent, less intelligent, less patriotic, and less hard-working than were "whites" as generic Americans undifferentiated by region.

Even if the jury is still out on what nonsoutherners really believe about the South, it is clear, as Reed no doubt suspected, that southerners throughout the South bracingly affirm their region, especially so in contrast to northerners. What,

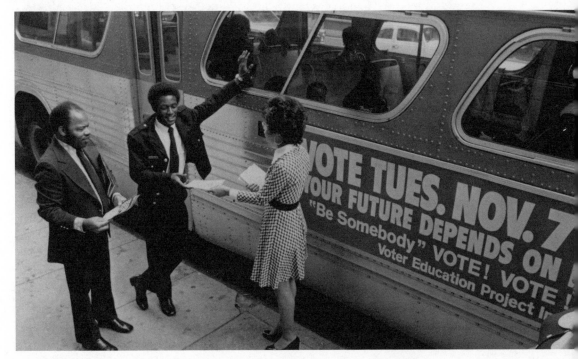

Whites and blacks both seem to become southerners—though probably not the same kind of southerners—largely in the same way, through the interplay of ascription and the social psychology of regionalism. A voter participation drive in Atlanta in 1973, from "The American South: Past, Present, and Future" exhibition at the Atlanta History Center, courtesy of the Atlanta History Center/Boyd Lewis Collection.

though, of the meat of his theory, that these beliefs influence southerners' self-proclaimed identities?

Southerners of both races who assert their region's superiority and positively stereotype it, who shun negative stereotypes, who ponder it in one way or another, and who are interested in the fate of their coregionalists and feel emotionally close to them tend strongly to use region as a point of reference in understanding and describing themselves (see Table 1). Eighty-eight percent of African Americans and 91 percent of whites who believe the South the best region in the country, for example, claim a southern identity. So, too, do 90 percent or so of both blacks and whites who feel close to other southerners. For these folks, whatever their race, it is almost impossible not to assert their southernness. Among whites, especially, some beliefs strongly distinguish self-labeled southerners from others in Dixie who choose, psychologically, to distance themselves from the South, at least as a marker of their personal identity: the "southern/nonsouthern" identity difference is 30 percent for those who champion the South as the nation's best region (91 percent v. 61 percent), 51 percent for those who discredit negative regional stereotypes (83 percent v. 32 percent), and 35 percent for those feeling close to other southerners (91 percent v. 56 percent).

Reed's views on regional identification thus appear vindicated, doubly so. Though he honed his theory on the history and culture of white southerners, he never suggested it should not apply to black southerners as well (or, for that matter, to other regional or social groups). As Table 1 shows, excepting only for perceptions of the "distinctiveness" of the South, African Americans' identity claims responded to regional social psychology in much the same way, if somewhat weaker, as do those of whites. Whites and blacks both seem to become southerners, then—though probably not the same kind of southerners—largely in the same way, through the interplay of ascription and the social psychology of regionalism.[11]

Again, Reed predicted these sorts of results, at least for whites. But they do not "prove" or even adequately demonstrate his theory because most of these social psychological motives to, or supports for, southern identification are also modestly influenced by longevity in the region, and residential history, in turn, is the strongest correlate of southern identity in the SFP. A third of lifelong southerners hold one or more negative stereotypes about the region; more than half of in-migrants do so. Likewise, if a southerner has lived exclusively in the region, she or he is more than 50 percent more likely than transplants to advance the South's superior regional status (64 percent for lifelong southerners v. 41 percent for migrants to the region). More sharply, only 19 percent of residents who have lived in the region less than five years feel close to other southerners; 55 percent of lifelong southerners feel so. Consequently, the patterns in Table 1 may simply reflect the impact of lifelong southern residency on both regional identity and regional

Table 1. Percent of Southerners Claiming a Southern Identity by Their Perceptions of the South

	Black		White	
	%	N	%	N
Distinctiveness of South (Fall 1991, Spring 1992, Fall 1993)				
South is like other parts of the U.S.	81	209	70	566
South is special and different	80	208	80	1,541
Regional Superiority of South (Fall 1991, Spring 1992, Fall 1993)				
South is not best region of the U.S.	72	178	61	834
South is best region/better than rest of U.S.	88	191	91	1,066
% of Positive Stereotypes Endorsed (Fall 1991, Spring 1992, Fall 1993, Fall 1995)				
Very few (40%)	71	88	55	323
Some (40–60%)	77	142	73	511
Many (60–80%)	82	110	76	638
Almost all/all (80–100%)	88	114	89	616
Number of Negative Stereotypes Endorsed (Fall 1993)				
0	80	44	83	334
1 (1 or more for African Americans)	75	32	78	148
2	—	—	37	59
3	—	—	32	25
Thought Given to South (Spring 1992, Fall 1992)				
Almost none	61	46	70	191
Only a little	76	29	64	247
Some	83	52	72	331
Quite a lot	87	63	81	493
Interest in Southerners' Success (Spring 1992, Fall 1992)				
Not much	69	36	60	262
Some	73	67	70	476
Great deal	89	80	85	494
Feelings of Closeness to Other Southerners (Spring 1992, Fall 1992, Fall 1999)				
Do not feel close/closer	68	170	56	965
Feel close	89	109	91	901

perceptions; if so, both the import of the latter and the utility of Reed's theory are exaggerated, possibly seriously so. The real test of his insights, then, requires taking the influence of residential history into account in efforts to gauge the independent role of sectional social psychology in transforming geography ("I live in the South") into identity ("I am a southerner"), or in severing the link between the two ("Though I have always lived in the South, I'm no southerner").

One instructive way to do this is to return to Reed's distinction between "assimilated nonsoutherners" and "lapsed southerners" and see if these beliefs about the South affect their identity choices. The first group, migrants to the region, is "at risk" of assimilating into a culture not initially their own by claiming a southern identity (51 percent do so); the second group of lifelong southerners is "at risk" of lapsing by rejecting a culture, or at least a label, that is theirs by birthright and residence (only 7 percent do so). So, psychologically, its easier to assimilate than to lapse, demonstrating yet again that ascription (by the individual and others) usually binds self to region. (We'll see this general principle in operation in Table 3 as well.) But do regional perceptions also matter for the self-proclaimed regional identities of assimilated and lapsed southerners?

Yes, clearly so, as Table 2 demonstrates. Migrants to the region who feel close to other southerners are two and a half times more likely to identify themselves

A large majority of lifelong southerners who do not feel especially close to other southerners still maintain a southern identity. Confederate shore batteries evoke the region's history at Fort Donelson National Military Park in Dover, Tennessee, courtesy of Tennessee Tourist Development.

Table 2. Percent Claiming or Rejecting a Southern Identity by Perceptions of the South: Individuals "at Risk" of Becoming Assimilated and Lapsed Southerners

	"At Risk" of Assimilation (Migrants to South)		"At Risk" of Lapsing (Life-Long Southern Residents)	
	% Who Claim Identity	N	% Who Reject Identity	N
Distinctiveness of South (Fall 1991, Spring 1992, Fall 1993)				
South is like other parts of the U.S.	46	302	9	490
South is special and different	55	656	6	1,132
Regional Superiority of South (Fall 1991, Spring 1992, Fall 1993)				
South is not best region of the U.S.	39	512	13	528
South is best region/better than rest of U.S.	73	355	4	939
% of Positive Stereotypes Endorsed (Fall 1991, Spring 1992, Fall 1993, Fall 1995)				
Less than 67%	42	561	9	711
67% or more	64	392	6	918
Number of Negative Stereotypes Endorsed (Fall 1993)				
2 or 3	20	65	22	27
0 or 1	56	155	6	380
Thought Given to South (Spring 1992, Fall 1992)				
Almost none/only a little/some	38	347	13	592
Quite a lot	55	212	5	366
Interest in Southerners' Success (Spring 1992, Fall 1992)				
Not much/some	38	357	14	525
Great deal	59	180	4	416
Feelings of Closeness to Other Southerners (Spring 1992, Fall 1992, Fall 1999)				
Do not feel close/closer	30	553	19	623
Feel close	74	270	3	760
Overall	51	5,719	7	10,557

as southern—that is, to assimilate—than those who lack such closeness (74 percent v. 30 percent). Similarly, lifelong southerners without this emotional attachment are six times more likely to lapse—to say "no" when asked if they are a southerner—than those who feel close to others in the region (19 percent v. 3 percent). Closeness to other southerners is only the most dramatic example of the causal force of regional social psychology. Lifelong southerners lapse almost four times more frequently if they believe two or three negative stereotypes about southerners than if they accept none or only one (22 percent v. 6 percent), and are three times more likely to do so if they believe the South no better than other parts of the country (13 percent v. 4 percent). In-migrants, on the other hand, are almost twice as likely as more skeptical transplants to assimilate by self-labeling as "southern" if they assert their new-found home's regional superiority (73 percent v. 39 percent).

Admittedly, these social psychological factors are neither necessary for one to believe oneself "southern," nor are they sufficient to do so. Ascription remains very potent. Note first, for example, the large majority of lifelong southerners who do not feel especially close to other southerners but who maintain a southern identity (19 percent reject the identity, 81 percent accept it), and, second, the large minority of newcomers to the region who, though accepting all or most of the positive stereotypes about the South, nevertheless refuse to define themselves as southerners (64 percent claim to be southern, 36 percent do not). Granting the huge impact of ascription on identity claims, each of these beliefs and perceptions nonetheless motivates in-migrants to assimilate, psychologically if not

Eudora Welty (here) once observed that "the Southerner. . . has got a character that does stem from his sense of place and of the significance of history and so on. . . . It's just a sense of continuity that has always characterized us, I think: a knowledge of family stories, that sense of generations and continuity. That gives us an identity." Photograph courtesy of the William R. Ferris Papers in Wilson Library's Southern Folklife Collection at the University of North Carolina at Chapel Hill.

necessarily behaviorally, by choosing to be a southerner and, though less power-fully and less universally, keeps lifelong southerners from lapsing by choosing to be "unsouthern."

Reed's insights, absolutely on the money so far, also imply that people are es-pecially enthusiastic about becoming or staying a southerner if they hold charac-teristics that they believe are typical of the region; that is, when they personally "fit" widely accepted (even informally enforced) regional stereotypes. Regional "misfits"—those who stereotype the South in particular ways (here, as accent-laden, politically conservative, and religious) but whose personal way of speaking, thinking, or acting contradicts the stereotypes (i.e., they are accent-free, moderate or liberal, and largely irreligious)—in turn should, if they are in-migrants, assimi-late less frequently and, if they are lifelong southerners, lapse more often. The residual category, or "free-thinkers," contains southerners who do not stereotype the South in any of these ways: whatever their personal traits (such as conserva-tive or liberal, speaking with an accent or not, etc.), they neither psychologically fit nor contradict the stereotype because, to them, it does not exist. This idea of regional "fit" quite obviously goes beyond mere perceptions about the region be-cause it incorporates how folks compare themselves to what they think are modal patterns around them.[12]

Reed's "fit" notion is supported, in one way or another, by each of the three

People, even if rooted in, and to, place, can choose to use region as a reference point for self-definition or not. Most southerners do. Photograph courtesy of Tennessee Tourist Development.

comparisons among geographic southerners (Table 3). "Misfits" uniformly define themselves as southern less frequently than do the "fits," who, also uniformly, exhibit the highest southern identification rates among the three groups. "Free-thinkers" generally fall between the two extremes. The "fits" apparently believe themselves to embody such regional stereotypes as conservatism and religiosity (stereotypes, again, that they themselves believe), and so they more readily integrate the South into their sense of who they are. Believing themselves outsiders to the region in which they live and have themselves stereotyped, "misfits," conversely, more often anchor their identities in places, things, or experiences other than the South.

Again, though, ascriptive factors such as residential history cloud matters: misfits, especially, are disproportionately northern transplants. But when I control in Table 3 for these confounding influences by looking at southerners at risk of assimilating (in-migrants) and of lapsing (lifelong southerners), we continue to see the same patterns. Transplants usually assimilate more often if their attitudes and behaviors match regional stereotypes, whether in terms of accent, conservatism, or religion. They are much less likely to think of themselves as southerners if they are "misfits." Newcomers who see the region as stamped by accents are especially unlikely to choose a southern identity if they believe themselves accent-free (only 20 percent do so). Likewise, lifelong southerners who "fit" regional stereotypes almost never lapse—only 3 to 5 percent do so. The "misfits" in this group, however, refuse to identify as southern at rates that are twice, three, even four times higher. "Free-thinkers" again usually occupy the middle position.[13]

Virtually every conjecture in Reed's trunk of regional insights was validated by what the Southern Focus Polls tell us about southerners and what they think about themselves and their region. No small feat, that. John Shelton Reed, photographed by Dan Sears, courtesy of News Services at the University of North Carolina at Chapel Hill.

Table 3. Percent Claiming or Rejecting a Southern Identity Among Respondents Whose Personal Characteristics or Beliefs Do or Do Not Match Their Stereotypes of the Region

	% of All Southerners Who Claim Identity	N	% of Migrants to South "At Risk" of Assimilation Who Claim Identity	N	% of Lifelong Southerners "At Risk" of Lapsing Who Reject Identity	N
A. Accent						
(Fall 1995)						
Fits	87	216	61	46	3	152
Free-thinkers	81	354	61	80	5	233
Misfits	43	142	20	76	14	50
B. Conservatism						
(Fall 1993)						
Fits	84	270	56	59	4	189
Free-thinkers	66	169	30	67	4	92
Misfits	69	309	46	112	11	170
C. Religion						
(Fall 1991, Spring 1992, Fall 1993, Fall 1995)						
Fits	82	1,533	56	445	5	1,043
Free-thinkers	73	970	49	357	8	568
Misfits	67	809	44	354	9	405

So, what do we make of all of this? Eudora Welty once observed that "the Southerner, the Mississippian, has got a character that does stem from his sense of place and of the significance of history and so on. . . . It's just a sense of continuity that has always characterized us, I think: a knowledge of family stories, that sense of generations and continuity. That gives us an identity."[14] Yes, place profoundly shapes who we are, and who we believe ourselves to be. None of this, however, necessarily need translate into an individual's or group's self-consciously articulated regional self-conceptions. People, even if rooted in, and to, place, can choose to use region as a reference point for self-definition or not. Most southerners do; a minority does not. By showing just how weighty is the social psychology of sectionalism in all of this, John Reed's ideas about regional identification help us understand with much greater clarity than previously the identity choices southerners make. Simply put, they'll opt to describe themselves—*understand* themselves—as southerners when they believe the South superior to other places and thus embrace its positive qualities and downplay its negative ones, see its distinctiveness from the hum-drum and the homogenized, reflect on its meaning, and identify and fit in with others in their region. Regional transplants more readily become assimilated nonsoutherners and lifelong residents more often avoid becoming lapsed southerners if this social psychology kicks in. And, as we saw from the Southern Focus Polls, for most in the region, black and white, it does indeed kick in. Virtually every conjecture in Reed's trunk of regional insights was validated by what these relatively recent, wonderfully rich, and geographically representative surveys tell us about southerners and what they think about themselves and their region. No small feat, that.

NOTES

I would like to thank Peggy Thoits, Kristin Gibson, Beth Latshaw, John Willis, and an anonymous reviewer for their helpful comments on this essay.

1. Henry Steele Commager, *The American Mind: An Interpretation of American Thought and Character Since the 1880s* (Yale University Press, 1950), 284–85; Henry Nash Smith, *Virgin Land: The American West as Symbol and Myth* (1950; rprt. Cambridge, 1970); Fred Hobson, *Tell About the South: The Southern Rage to Explain* (Louisiana State University Press, 1983), 9; C. Vann Woodward, "The Search for Southern Identity," in Woodward, *The Burden of Southern History*, rev. ed. (Louisiana State University Press, 1968), 3–25; Sanford Levinson, *Written in Stone: Public Monuments in Changing Societies* (Duke University Press, 1998), 31; Carl Degler, "Thesis, Antithesis, Synthesis: The South, the North, and the Nation," *Journal of Southern History* 53 (February 1987): 3–18; Larry J. Griffin, "Southern Distinctiveness, Yet Again; Or, Why America Still Needs the South," *Southern Cultures* 6 (Fall 2000): 51–76; J. Bill Berry, "The Southern Autobiographical Impulse," *Southern Cultures* 6 (Spring 2000): 7.

2. Larry J. Griffin, "Why Was the South a Problem to America?" in *The South as an American Problem*, ed. Larry J. Griffin and Don H. Doyle (University of Georgia Press, 1995), 10–32; Sheldon Hackney, "The Contradictory South," *Southern Cultures* 7 (Winter 2001): 65–80; Jack Temple Kirby, *Media-Made Dixie: The South in American Imagination* (Louisiana State University Press, 1978); Allison Graham, *Framing the South: Hollywood, Television, and Race During the Civil Rights Struggle* (Johns Hopkins University Press, 2001). That individuals develop a group, especially racial, identity because of the imposition of that identity on them by others is well documented. See, for example, George J. Sánchez, *Becoming Mexican-American: Ethnicity, Culture, and Identity in Chicano Los Angeles, 1900–1945* (Oxford University Press, 1993), and Mia Tuan, *Forever Foreigners or Honorary Whites: The Asian Experience Today* (Rutgers University Press, 2003).

3. John Shelton Reed, *Southerners: The Social Psychology of Sectionalism* (University of North Carolina Press, 1983), 14.

4. Reed, *Southerners*, 14; Larry J. Griffin, Ranae J. Evenson, and Ashley B. Thompson, "Southerners All?" *Southern Cultures* 11 (Spring 2005): 6–25. The Southern Focus Polls were sponsored by the University of North Carolina and the Atlanta *Journal Constitution*.

5. Reed, *Southerners*, 23, 20. From what we call tell from the SFP, most self-defined southerners do not see their southern identity displacing a broader American identity. When asked in the Spring 1994 and Fall 1994 SFP whether being a southerner or being an American "means more to" respondents, 91 percent of those said "American," 3.5 percent reported "depends," and fewer than 6 percent said "southern."

6. Reed, *One South: An Ethnic Approach to Regional Culture* (Louisiana State University Press, 1982); Herbert Gans, "Symbolic Ethnicity: The Future of Ethnic Groups and Cultures in America," *Ethnic and Racial Studies* 2.1 (1979): 1–20; John Egerton, *The Americanization of Dixie: the Southernization of America* (Harper's Magazine Press, 1974); Larry J. Griffin and Ashley B. Thompson, "Enough About the Disappearing South, What About the Disappearing Southerner?" *Southern Cultures* 9 (Fall 2003): 51–65.

7. Reed's most forceful expression of his views on the regional identification process is found in "The Sociology of Regional Groups," in *One South*, 11–32. (The quote is on p. 16.) See also Reed, *The Enduring South: Subcultural Persistence in Mass Society* (1972; University of North Carolina Press, 1986), and Reed, "Southerners as an American Ethnic Group," in Reed, *"My Tears Spoiled My Aim" and Other Reflections on Southern Culture* (Harcourt Brace, 1994), 29–41. Historian George Tindall and sociologist Lewis M. Killian were exploring the ethnic analogy at about the same time as Reed. See Tindall, "Beyond the Mainstream: The Ethnic Southerners," in Tindall, *The Ethnic Southerners* (Louisiana State University Press, 1976), 1–21, and Killian, *White Southerners*, rev. ed. (University of Massachusetts Press, 1985). Paralleling Reed, other social psychologists were also developing similar understandings of group identity. See, especially, Henri Tajfel, "Social Categorization, Social Identity and Social Comparison," in Tajfel, ed., *Differentiation between Social Groups: Studies in the Social Psychology of Intergroup Relations* (Academic Press, 1978), 61–76, and John C. Turner, Penelope J. Oakes, S. Alexander Haslam, and Craig McGarty, "Self and Collective: Cognition and Social Context," *Personality and Social Psychology Bulletin* 20.5 (1994): 454–63. An exceptionally rich contribution to the study of ethnic identity is Joane Nagel, "Constructing Ethnicity: Creating and Recreating Ethnic Identity and Culture," *Social Problems* (February 1994): 152–76.

8. Some of Reed's arguments are addressed with the SFP data, albeit with a greatly different focus, in Larry J. Griffin, "Whiteness and Southern Identity in the Mountain and Lowland South," *Journal of Appalachian Studies* 10 (Spring/Fall 2004): 7–37.

9. For stereotypes used in Reed, *Southerners* (e.g., religious, friendly), I scored them as he did. For other characteristics, I scored them according to my understandings of what most Americans would likely consider positive and negative traits of southerners. Data from the nationally representative 1990 General Social Survey, based on a large nationally representative sample of adults, largely validated my sense of regional stereotypes. The General Social Survey is fielded by the National Opinion Research Center at the University of Chicago. See http://webapp.icpsr.umich.edu/GSS/index.html (accessed 5 April 2006).

10. Throughout these analyses, whites and African Americans may be of Hispanic or non-Hispanic origin. There were too few respondents of other races (e.g., Asian, Native American) in the southern samples for separate presentation.

11. White and black southerners differ substantially in their assessments of the meaning of Confederate symbols such as the battle flag, vote for different political parties, hold different views on racial policies such as affirmative action, evaluate the moral dimension of the southern past differentially, and do not share the same collective memories of American and southern history. See, for example, Griffin, "Whiteness and Southern Identity in the Mountain and Lowland South," and Larry J. Griffin, "'Generations and Collective Memory Revisited: Race, Region, and Memory of Civil Rights," *American Sociological Review* 69 (August 2005): 544–57. An anonymous reviewer correctly pointed out that regional social psychology may be a consequence of regional identification rather than its cause, as I, following Reed, assume. If this is true, my results should be interpreted with caution. Unraveling fully whether identity causes the social psychology of sectionalism, or regional social psychology shapes identity, requires longitudinal data, in which the same respondents are surveyed at least twice. With such data, for example, I could determine

if the social psychology of sectionalism at an earlier time shaped later regional identity choices. Unfortunately, the SFPs are not longitudinal; instead, they yield cross-sectional data in which attitudes and identity are assessed in the same survey.

12. Respondents were defined as "fitting" these normative regional attributes if they claimed that southerners were a) more conservative than residents of other regions and they, themselves, were conservative, or b) more religious and they, themselves, reported attending church at least several times a month, or c) were marked by accents and they, themselves, believed they spoke with at least a detectable southern accent. Conservative fit was ascertained from the Fall 1993 SFP; accent fit from the Fall 1995 SFP; and religious fit from the Fall 1991, Spring 1992, Fall 1993, and Fall 1995 SFPs. The questions necessary to determine fit were not asked in any other SFP.

13. That such a large percentage of "free-thinkers" about the accent stereotype claim to be southern is testament, yet again, to the power of ascriptive characteristics in molding social identity. More than two-thirds of "free-thinkers" believe themselves to speak "southern" and that, in and of itself, is almost as important as personally matching a regional stereotype. Religious fit's impact on identity claims is not limited to religious observance per se: it is evident, as well, when fit is defined in terms of values. Eighty-two percent of southerners in the Fall 1993 SFP who stereotype the South as more religious and who also say that religion is "very important" in their own lives (as opposed to "fairly" or "not very" important) self-categorize as southern; only 46 percent of those who share the stereotype but not the personal value ("misfits") do so. Were I to add Protestantism as another criterion in determining religious "fits" and "misfits"—a plausible strategy given its cultural significance in the region—the effect of religious fit on self-definition would be shown to be even greater than presented in Table 3. On the intermingling of Protestantism and southernness, see Reed, "The Sociology of Regional Groups"; Samuel S. Hill Jr., *Southern Churches in Crisis* (Holt, Rinehart and Wilson, 1967), 23; Hill, "Introduction," in Samuel S. Hill Jr., with Edgar T. Thompson, Anne Firor Scott, Charles Hudson, and Edwin S. Gaustad, *Religion and the Solid South* (Abingdon Press, 1972); and Griffin, et al., "Southerners All?"

14. Quoted in Nancy Dorman-Hickson, review of *Eudora Welty: A Writer's Life*, by Ann Waldron. *Southern Living* (February 1999). See http://www.findarticles.com/p/articles/mi_qa3676/is_199902/ai_n8829136 (accessed 5 April 2006).

"The Boys Will Have to Fight the Battles without Me"
The Making of Sam Davis, "Boy Hero of the Confederacy"

by Edward John Harcourt

Executed as a spy in 1863, Sam Davis would be memorialized as the Confederate "boy hero" by the Lost Cause movement. Today, Davis's boyhood home is a popular Tennessee tourist attraction. A Sam Davis reenactor at the Sam Davis Home, courtesy of the Rutherford County Convention and Visitors Bureau.

On a recent Confederate Memorial Day at the Tennessee State Capitol, the General Joseph E. Johnston Camp No. 28, Sons of Confederate Veterans (SCV), performed a pathetic little ceremony under the portico of the antebellum building. A small band of die-hards, their numbers were more than doubled by curious tourists, conscripted children, and an entertainment troupe called the Dixie Picks. A history professor from a local community college began proceedings with an angry and passionate recitation of Father Abram Joseph Ryan's poem to the battle flag. Turning southwards, the speaker pointed to the statue of the Confederate martyr Sam Davis, erected on Capitol grounds in 1909, and proclaimed that the story of the "boy hero" was "a living reminder of the valor of your flesh and blood." Executed by the Union army in 1863 for scouting behind enemy lines, Sam Davis had become a folk hero by the end of the nineteenth century; almost Christ-like in his representation of duty, bravery, and honor, he embodied the South's idealized image of itself during the crisis of the 1860s.

The martyr's honor, however, was besieged at the turn of the twenty-first century by those who wished to associate the memory of his "matchless glory" with the shame of slavery. Within fifteen feet of the Confederate statue, the speaker's friends had thrown a tarpaulin over a simple monument erected in 1999 by the Black Caucus of Tennessee state legislators to the victims of the Middle Passage who died en route to slavery in the Americas. The dedication of this simple granite block, set beside a Scarlet Oak sapling, had infuriated members of the SCV who called the monument's proximate placement to the Davis statue "a foolish little sophomoric prank." In a testy exchange of opinions in the press, a spokesperson for the Black Caucus claimed no intent "to disrespect a Confederate soldier or have it overshadow him in any way" and said that that the location for the monument to slavery's victims was determined by horticultural factors alone. Nonetheless, on Confederate Memorial Day the monument was covered to erase any suggestion that slavery was part of the secessionists' cause.[1]

Once a defiant public celebration for southern whites, Confederate Memorial Day has never been a moment for ambivalent thinking about southern identity and the meaning of the Civil War. The days when governors eulogized the Confederate cause, and the most prominent citizens jockeyed for position on the speaker's podium, are long gone. But though the crowds no longer come, time has not diluted the moral imperative — the passionate certitude — of Confederate symbolism, which, like Corinthian columns, continues to dominate the temple of the South's historical imagination. As readers of *Southern Cultures* are well aware, however, the white South's public commemoration of the Civil War era tells a highly selective, carefully orchestrated, and incomplete story of the service, suffering, and sacrifice of Americans during the terrible crisis of the 1860s. In recent years, scholars of the American Civil War era — taking a cue from historians of the First World War and the Holocaust—have moved into the study of historical memory both to explore how we have come to know what we think happened during the 1860s and to reconceptualize the questions we ask about one of the most critical events in U.S. history. In a southern context, the move into memory studies seems especially appropriate because so many popular assumptions and sources about the war and its aftermath continue to be stained with a resilient dye of sentimentalism, white supremacy, and martial nostalgia.[2]

The commemorative history of Sam Davis is a case study in collective memory making as part of the reconstruction of white southern identity during the late nineteenth and early twentieth centuries; these memories and identities, moreover, are sustained and perpetuated today by many white southerners. There is a puzzling lack of ambiguity in the commemoration of Davis. Given the seismic changes in society over the past fifty years, why has it proven to be so difficult to reinterpret Davis's image in ways that would allow other historical narratives to play a part? Tracing the development of the Sam Davis memory cult from autobiographical reminiscences to state-sponsored shrines offers a closer understanding of the immutability of Confederate history and of the problem of historical representation that prevents the modern South from coming to terms with the complexity of its troubled past. As historian David Blight has observed, if Americans are to understand the shape and silences of their Civil War inheritance, and to grasp the difficulty of imposing ambivalent meanings onto the past, then "how some selections become or remain dominant, taking on mythic dimensions, and others do not is the tale to be told."[3]

What is most striking about the heroic response to tragedy at the heart of the Sam Davis story is the absence of fabrication or embellishment. To some degree, this would come later, but the earliest accounts of Davis's martyrdom are rooted unambiguously in historical sources authored by Union agents. The story we can recover from these sources goes like this: On November 27, 1863, on a scaffold outside Pulaski in Middle Tennessee, the Union army executed Sam Davis, a twenty-one year-old Confederate scout attached to the Army of Tennessee. Davis had been one of at least forty-five scouts detailed for special, hazardous duty within the Union lines of occupation around Nashville. At the time of his arrest by Union secret service agents, Davis had in his possession a miscellany of newspapers and intelligence sources, which included detailed drawings of Union fortifications at Nashville and other towns in Middle Tennessee. Imprisoned in Pulaski, which at that time was a garrisoned Union town under command of General Grenville M. Dodge, Davis faced charges of espionage and steadfastly refused to reveal the names of his informants. After his prisoner was found guilty, General Dodge, as noted by a newspaper correspondent for the Cincinnati *Daily Commercial* present at the scene, announced that Davis should be hanged on a hill described by the reporter as "a pretty eminence, north east of Pulaski, and

Erected almost a hundred years ago, the statue of Sam Davis continues to be a focus of Confederate remembrance. A contemporary postcard of the statue (left), Southern Latex Co., Nashville, and photograph of crowd assembled at the 1909 dedication (below) from Confederate Veteran *XVII (June 1909), reproduced courtesy of the Rare Book, Manuscript, and Special Collections Library, Duke University, Durham, North Carolina.*

overlooking the town." When local citizens protested at so visual a display of a gruesome act, Dodge replied, "I want him hung where you all can see him. There are more of you guilty of his crime—I know it—and if I ever get my hands upon you, d––n you, I'll hang you upon the same gallows." According to the newspaper story, which is corroborated by several eyewitness accounts recorded between 1863 and the 1890s, Dodge offered Davis his life in exchange for information about his informants. The condemned man apparently refused all such offers. "Would *you* betray a friend?" Davis is reported to have said while seated on his coffin. "I had rather die a thousand deaths." Confederate lore had Davis saying upon climbing the scaffold that "The boys will have to fight the battles without me."[4]

Bearing his fate bravely, Davis apparently touched upon the sympathies of all observers, including his captors. The reporter recorded the scene thus:

All nature seemed to be in mourning, and many warm hearts, loyal and true, but more that were not, melted into sympathy. Four companies of the 111th Illinois and two companies of the 7th Iowa were drawn up, forming a hollow square with fixed bayonets, with the gallows in the center of it. Hundreds and thousands were the spectators; the soldiery paraded about the guard; the citizens, gazing with scowls from their dwellings.

The Provost Marshal took off the prisoner's hat, for his hands were tied behind him, and then Chaplain Young, of the 81st Ohio, addressed a throne of mercy in behalf of his soul. And that prayer—it was long and fervently prayed that if a reprieve was not to be given on earth, that a higher, better, lasting one might be given in Heaven, where wars come not. Then he implored God's blessing upon our whole country—that sweet peace might soon return again—that the time when war should no longer be waged might come even speedily; and every breathing heart in that vast multitude said, "Amen!"

After a white hood was tied over the prisoner's head, the trap door was sprung at 10:30 that morning. Union soldiers turned away as Davis writhed in death agony for three minutes. "He stood it like a man," one Union soldier noted in his diary the following day. "He never paled a bit but stood it like a hero." That night, the *Daily Commercial* reported, "evergreens were planted, and now sigh in the wild wintery winds o'er his grave, while flowers culled by fair hands, were strewn upon it."[5]

This tragic tale was not that unusual for the time and place. Sam Davis suffered a fate shared by many intelligence gatherers operating around Nashville, which had been under Union occupation since February 1862 and had quickly become a central Union depot for the western theater. Most of the rural counties surrounding Nashville were only nominally under Union control, and this "no-man's land" witnessed over three years of bloody internecine conflict and the steady dissolution of the institution of slavery. In this context, execution for espionage was not uncommon. "Spies are hung every now and then," commented James Fremantle, a British journalist traveling with the Confederate General Braxton Bragg's command in the summer of 1863. The Provost Marshall records for Middle Tennessee offer evidence of scores of executions on espionage charges, with not all the victims receiving trials. Six months before Davis's execution, Union commanders publicly executed Joseph Smith in Carthage, a rural town east of Nashville. The following month two Confederate spies who had posed as federal officers were hanged in Franklin, twenty miles south of Nashville. As was the case with Davis, some of these events generated newspaper coverage and featured in private letters. In January 1864, a Confederate spy named Dodd was executed near Knoxville, and before ascending the gallows he too wrote his relatives what one journalist described as a "touching and yet manly letter." Most executions, however, went unrecorded apart from a perfunctory note in the Provost Marshall's records.[6]

Today, over six generations later, the lives of all of these men are almost entirely forgotten—all except Sam Davis. By the early twentieth century, the story of Davis's death had become a celebrated instance in the culture of Confederate remembrance and a centerpiece of Lost Cause commemoration shared and sustained by communities of historical memory in Tennessee. Today, representa-

Union commanding officer General Grenville M. Dodge was determined to use Davis's execution as an example to others: "I want him hung where you all can see him," he declared. "There are more of you guilty of his crime—I know it—and if I ever get my hands upon you, d——n you, I'll hang you upon the same gallows." Wartime photograph of Dodge, courtesy of the Collections of the Library of Congress.

tions of the life and death of Sam Davis mark the historical and geographical landscapes of the Middle Tennessee heartland. Monuments commemorating him stand at the scene of his execution and on the court square in Pulaski; at his childhood home outside Smyrna, Tennessee; and in the form of a life-size statue positioned prominently on the southeast corner of the state capitol grounds in Nashville. An exhibition case of Sam Davis artifacts—including the overcoat worn at the time of his arrest and the boot in which papers were concealed—is on permanent display at the Tennessee State Museum. (The boot is listed among a dozen "top artifacts" for children to explore at the museum. Other items include Daniel Boone's musket, David Crockett's powder horn, a mastadon jawbone discovered in Tennessee, and James K. Polk's walking cane.) Over the years archivists at the Tennessee State Library and Archives have procured and cataloged scores of documents: firsthand recollections, poems, commemorative speeches, at least four published biographies, and the papers of the Sam Davis Memorial Association (SDMA). Each year, thousands of visitors—the majority local school children—visit the Sam Davis Home outside Smyrna, which for nearly seventy-five years has been owned and maintained by the State of Tennessee through the SDMA. Since the late 1890s, Davis has towered above any other Tennessean in the pantheon of Confederate Civil War heroes.[7]

TO RESCUE FROM OBLIVION

Sam Davis was not always so famous, however. For nearly thirty years after the war, the story of his execution rested in private realms, the flame of memory tended only by family and close friends. The execution had gained some notoriety at the time, especially among soldiers of the Army of Tennessee. Writing in the early 1880s, Private Sam Watkins recalled that in 1864 his regiment had assembled to watch the hanging of two young Yankee spies, eager to see the condemned men suffer because "they had hung one of our regiment at Pulaski—Sam Davis." In 1866 Davis's father erected the first monument to his son, a twenty-five foot shaft of Italian marble, at the back of the family's plantation home outside Smyrna. In the 1870s and 1880s the story appeared briefly in publications chronicling the wartime service of the Army of Tennessee. Opinion did not always agree, however, on the story's merits. While J. B. Killebrew, a noted state official, praised the young Confederate's heroism, a sketch of the story in the 1886 *Goodspeed* history of Giles County noted that "opinion is divided as to whether the doomed man was really a brave man, and sought death rather than divulge a friend's name, or whether he was playing for glory, even in his last moments." Such observations were soon to become blasphemous.[8]

The Sam Davis story became part of a broader social memory only in the mid-1890s and chiefly through the efforts of Sumner Archibald Cunningham, the founding editor of *Confederate Veteran* magazine. Marked by the institutionalization of Jim Crow across the South, the 1890s, described by C. Vann Woodward as a "twilight zone between living memory and written history," also witnessed in a parallel process the maturation of Lost Cause mythology in southern culture and an increasing spirit of reconciliation between North and South. In their recreation of their shared historical past, former Confederates soothed the wounds of recent history by producing what Allen Tate called "a sentimental literature of narcissism, in which the South tried to define itself by looking into a glass behind its back." White southerners were assisted in this effort by northern novelists and publishers eager to transform the antebellum South into a romantic idyll of brave men, elegant women, and loyal slaves. At the same time, the soldiers of secessionism were cast as honorable and unrepentant defenders of states' rights in the face of northern aggression. Sumner Cunningham became one of the key cultural players in this drama. A native of Middle Tennessee, Cunningham had an undistinguished record of Confederate service. In the opinion of his biographer, he had the distinction "to be absent from the ranks on the eves of impending battles to an extent that approached desertion." Following defeat at the Battle of Nashville in December 1864, he returned home to Bedford County and effectively deserted Confederate service. After the war Cunningham worked at various newspaper jobs before becoming the general agent for the Jefferson Davis Memorial Fund after the former Confederate president's death in 1889. He left this position shortly after launching the Nashville-based *Confederate Veteran* in January 1893. The publication struggled financially in its early years, becoming solvent only after its adoption as the official organ of the United Confederate Veterans.[9]

Before starting *Confederate Veteran*, Cunningham had never heard of Sam Davis. When an early subscriber submitted a school oration about Davis for publication, Cunningham rejected it, "feeling that there were so many equally worthy heroes it would hardly be fair to print this special eulogy." But at a Blue-Gray reunion in April 1895 on the battlefield at Shiloh, Cunningham again heard the story of Davis's execution—this time from two federal veterans, witnesses to the execution, who claimed, as Cunningham phrased it, that "the Federal Army was in grief over it." This account struck a chord and convinced Cunningham of the merits of publicizing the story. The Union veterans' story of an ordinary soldier's heroic death, couched in the language of reconciliation, fit perfectly with the spirit of the times and the viewpoint of the *Confederate Veteran*. Publication would also further Cunningham's desire to propagate the story of the ordinary common soldier, in part to reach a mass audience. "I resolved to print the story," Cunningham recalled in 1899, "and [to] reprint it until that typical hero should have as full credit as the *Veteran* could give him."[10]

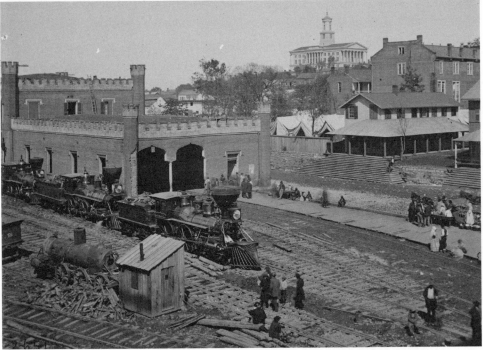

Under Union occupation, Nashville served as a depot for the Civil War's western theater. A view of wartime Nashville from the steps of the state capitol (above) and the railroad yard (below), both courtesy of the Collections of the Library of Congress.

As Cunningham assumed stewardship of the Sam Davis story, he transformed the oral memories of Middle Tennessee natives and federal veterans into a broad collective memory through a series of extemporizations and promotions. First, he solicited written versions of the federal eyewitness accounts of Davis's execution that he had heard at the Shiloh reunion and then published them in the *Veteran*. J. A. M. Collins, veteran of the Second Iowa Volunteer Infantry, recounted the execution and wrote that, although the execution was justified under military law, Davis should have been given a "true soldier['s]" death by firing squad. Nonetheless, Collins remembered "the glorious manner" in which Davis met his death, citing the "thrice-refused" offer on the scaffold to accept a reprieve in return for information. Calling Davis an example "of the highest type of American manhood," Collins remembered that the execution was "regretted not alone by Confederates, but by every soldier in our line who was capable of appreciating a noble nature."[11]

Next, Cunningham called for Tennesseans to come forward with "such data as may be recalled by all who know anything of the event." He was swamped by correspondence from interested readers, one of whom wrote, "You can do your state and country no better service than to rescue from oblivion the name of Sam Davis." The letter writer's conclusion points to Davis's growing importance to the Confederate heritage movement: "The thought of him brings back to us . . . the flaming spirit of self-reliance and self-sacrifice which made those years vivid with a glory deathless as man's love of virtue." Other comments also revealed the eagerness of Cunningham's readers to reach back into the past to fashion stories that glorified and commemorated the sacrifices of ordinary soldiers.[12]

Sensing an opportunity to galvanize interest in his fledgling publication, Cunningham abandoned his plans to organize a monument to Otho F. Strahl, the Confederate general killed at the Battle of Franklin, and threw his energies into sponsorship of Sam Davis's story. In a series of editorials published in the summer of 1895, Cunningham packaged Davis's sacrifice in Christian terms, insisting that the story had "never been excelled in the history of man." "In faith to principle," he added, "it is almost divine, and recalls even the sacrifice of the Galilean whose hands and feet were nailed to a cross." By summer's end, Cunningham launched a fundraising drive for a monument to Davis's memory to be erected on the Tennessee State Capitol grounds in Nashville and announced that November 27—the thirty-second anniversary of the soldier's death—would be the deadline for a fundraising and subscription drive. In subsequent issues Cunningham printed the name of every subscriber to the fund and kept the story of Sam Davis before his audience, with poems, eyewitness accounts of his execution, and recollections of Sam Davis as a boy and soldier gracing each issue.[13]

Commemorations of Sam Davis are evident across Middle Tennessee: from statues and markers to the Sam Davis Home (pictured here), which attracts thousands of schoolchildren and other visitors each year. Both photographs courtesy of the Rutherford County Convention and Visitors Bureau.

Why was Cunningham so fascinated with Sam Davis's story? Perhaps he found in Davis redemption for his own lackluster military performance, but he also believed that "never was there such an opportunity for Confederates to establish through the press so much in their honor as now." At Shiloh in 1895 Cunningham heard expressions of fraternal greeting that convinced him that the time had arrived to bring Confederate heroism to the fore. Enmities were receding as the years passed, but white northern veterans also shared similar challenges to their racial identities from aliens in their midst. Cunningham, writing in the *Veteran*, gave an account of one northern soldier's views: "The race problem is a sore one; that, you people will have to settle yourselves, while we have a worse one in having to deal with the Anarchist element coming in a continuous stream from other lands, and we feel we may have to look to you of the South in the threatened emergency." Cunningham characterized this opinion as "politics without reference to party," but in reality it was about whiteness without reference to race. Cunningham also believed he was referring to reunion without reference to region, but in reality he brought a distinctively southern and Confederate sensibility to his encounters with his old friends, the enemy. As historian Grace Hale has observed of this period, southern whites developed identities around two juxtapositions: that of ex–Confederates against ex-slaves, and of the South against the nation. Sam Davis was more virtuous than a Yankee and more loyal than a slave: he was the perfect embodiment of a white southern racial fantasy for the 1890s.[14]

For Tennesseans, the Sam Davis story filled a need for the neo–Confederates who wanted to memorialize the state's ill-fated and catastrophic move to secede from the Union. Nathan Bedford Forrest was the closest thing Tennessee had to a genuine Civil War hero, but his image, while powerful, was compromised by his record of trading in slaves before the war, his role in the massacre of colored Union troops at Fort Pillow, and his participation in the Ku Klux Klan movement of the late 1860s. Neo–Confederates such as Albert Virgil Goodpasture, a state official, and William R. Garrett, a historian, whose *History of Tennessee* was widely adopted in public schools, ran into heated debates with critics about the amount of space devoted to Forrest in their account of the Civil War. Compared with the imperfect image of Forrest, then, Sam Davis was an unblemished and uncomplicated subject for a whitewashed Confederate remembrance.[15]

The positive response to Cunningham's appeal came from a number of quarters—some of them from far outside the inner circle of Confederate memorialization. In a powerful demonstration of the role of the Lost Cause myth as a civil religion, Jefferson Davis's widow, Varina Howell Davis, agreed that "the dear boy *who died for his faith* should be forever beloved and held in tender memory by us all." Other prominent Confederates, including John B. Gordon and J. William Jones, wrote to the *Confederate Veteran* in support. Although donors to the monument fund were overwhelmingly from the former Confederacy, a number of Union veterans also contributed. Captain H. I. Smith of Mason City, Iowa, sent a contribution in honor of a Yankee comrade killed at Corinth, Mississippi. Astonishingly, the Union officials who superintended the execution of Davis also responded to Cunningham's plea, including General Dodge, who sent Cunningham a copy of Davis's trial transcript as well as a contribution to the monument fund. Dodge wrote in a letter he had had several Confederate spies executed "who were equally brave in meeting their fate," so he appreciated "fully that the people of the South and Davis's comrades understand his soldierly qualities and propose to honor his memory." The Reverend James Young, the Union chaplain who had tended the condemned man on the eve of the execution and recited the benediction at the scaffold, sent Cunningham the dyed Union overcoat that Davis was wearing at the time of his arrest; he had been given the overcoat by Davis, he wrote, who requested him "to keep it in remembrance of him." In turning it over to the *Veteran*, the elderly chaplain considered "the remembrance fairly fulfilled." Unlike the Romans, this gesture implied, the Yankees returned the cloaks of their victims.[16]

Despite the overwhelming response from correspondents, after several months Cunningham had raised only $400 toward the erection of a monument, most of it from Tennesseans. In efforts to raise additional funds, Cunningham encouraged readers of his magazine to send spare dimes, and he organized in May 1896 a graveside memorial service at the Davis home in Smyrna, to which more than one thousand people came. Other supporters were even more enterprising. W. D. Fox of Murfreesboro wrote a stage play about the martyred Confederate and, together with a makeshift drama troupe, performed the drama throughout Middle Tennessee. Another promoter developed a board game, "The Game of Confederate Heroes," and donated the proceeds to the cause. Upon hearing the story, schoolteachers at white public schools sponsored essay contests and, with Cunningham's encouragement, a few organized Sam Davis clubs and debating teams. For his own efforts, Cunningham sold miniature statues of Davis at the Tennessee Centennial Exposition in 1897, where a "spirited bust of that faithful young hero of the South" featured prominently in the Confederate Exhibit, next to the sword, pistol, and sash of General Forrest.[17]

Cunningham found perhaps the most willing and devoted allies for his cause in the Daughters of the Confederacy, a Nashville-based group who helped found the United Daughters of the Confederacy (UDC) in 1895. A meeting that year between Cunningham and the Nashville UDC suggests the emotional power that collective memories of Davis evoked among sympathetic audiences. Before

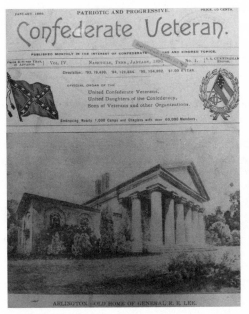

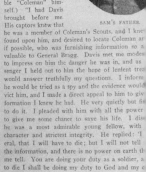

As Lost Cause mythology emerged in full force during the 1890s, Sumner Archibald Cunningham launched Confederate Veteran magazine. It would become an influential mouthpiece for celebrations of the Old South and its heroes—including Sam Davis. Cover of the January 1896 issue (left) and detail from an article about Sam Davis in the June 1909 issue (right), both reproduced courtesy of the Rare Book, Manuscript, and Special Collections Library, Duke University, Durham, North Carolina.

speaking, Cunningham presented Sam Davis's overcoat, which he had recently received from the Union chaplain. The minutes of the meeting, as reported by Cunningham in the *Veteran*, recorded a remarkable performance: "When it was shown every heart was melted to tears, and there we sat in that sacred silence. Not a sound was heard save the sobs that came from aching hearts. It was a time too sacred for words, for we seemed almost face to face with that grand and heroic man. . . . With one accord we wept together; and it was some time before we could resume business."[18]

The commemoration of Davis as a Confederate hero provided a useful analog to the historical narrative of Confederate womanhood for the self-styled daughters of the Confederacy. This ordinary soldier's youth, valor, self-sacrifice, and devotion to cause were virtues that featured prominently in Lost Cause stories about Confederate women during the war. But though the women identified with Davis, his story in the hands of the Daughters became one of "manly virtue" and an exercise in restoring honor to the defeated white men of the South while conveying that honor to their sons. In a remarkably graphic image of the power of print to affect remembered experience, Sally Ivie of Murfreesboro, Tennessee, in the late 1890s took her Civil War diary from the 1860s and transformed it into a scrapbook of Civil War memories for her son—retitling her diary "Confederate Veteran" by pasting a copy of the cover page of Cunningham's *Confederate Veteran* onto the cover. The diary entries inside the volume were effaced by newspaper stories from the 1890s, including a feature article on Sam Davis. A commemorative history created out of stories of valor, heroism, and sacrifice was what Sally Ivie wanted her son to read, not her original thoughts and notations from the 1860s, most of which she apparently wished to forget.[19]

The effort to commemorate Davis was also simultaneously an exercise in forgetting. Davis's memory eclipsed the deep ambivalence many Tennesseans felt about the Confederacy's rebellion. It erased the less-than-honorable service of thousands of white men, including Cunningham, who had deserted the Army of Tennessee, and in making Davis the epitome of virtue, it foreclosed on the public space for the commemoration of African American struggles—particularly those of men who had escaped slavery and served honorably in the Union army. While this was going on, Tennessee passed a secret ballot law, a Poll Tax, and literacy tests in order to disfranchise African Americans. But it wasn't enough to purge blacks from political life. A segregated society also required a segregated history, and though African Americans in Middle Tennessee continued in private spaces to commemorate the heritage of emancipation throughout the darkest days of segregation, the memorialization of Davis' story contained a cultural power that trumped all other competing narratives in the region's collective consciousness.

As the Sam Davis project gained momentum, Cunningham joined forces with veterans' groups and Tennessee legislators to bring his monument to fruition. Adding to the drive to secure donations from other states, the State of Tennessee eventually appropriated $5,000 for the monument and appointed Cunningham head of a committee to choose an appropriate site on the Capitol grounds. The treasurer of the committee was John C. Kennedy, the man that the Davis family had sent to retrieve their son's body from the shallow grave outside of Pulaski in 1863. The committee resolved to raise money from every state in the Union and to make the monument "a presentation to the youth of all America" of "what one American soul of heroic mould [could do] even when encased in the body of a mere boy." Notices were placed in newspapers across the Union and appeals sent to northern veterans' associations. The fundraising effort was easier in some states than in others. From the Office of the Adjutant General in Des Moines, a veteran of the 2nd Iowa Infantry enquired, "Is not this the man who went to his death at Pulaski? . . . If this is the one I think it is, I haven't the least idea but what nearly every one of the regiment to which I belong would be willing to subscribe a small amount." But by the close of 1908, seventeen states—all outside the South—had failed to respond. Appeals to governors and congressmen followed, and on January 25 Representative Albert V. Locke of New Hampshire sent a personal check to complete the roster of all states in the Union. Unveiled on the capitol grounds on April 29, 1909, the monument depicts Davis in a defiant posture, his arms crossed and head tilted slightly backward looking south.

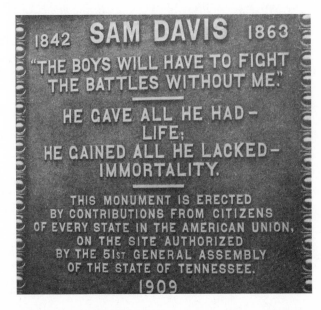

By the time the monument was unveiled in 1909, the committee had succeeded in collecting donations from every state of the Union. The statue of Sam Davis exemplified the process of sectional reconciliation through an idealized memory of the Civil War. Monument dedication, pictured in Confederate Veteran *XVII (June 1909), reproduced courtesy of the Rare Book, Manuscript, and Special Collections Library, Duke University, Durham, North Carolina.*

The Tennessee governor delivered a eulogy. In an editorial the following day, the *Tennessean* underscored the broader meaning of the statue's unveiling, commemorating both a cause, "though lost, still just," and a civilization, "the Old South, whose son he was."[20]

Shortly after the statue was erected, the Tennessee UDC arranged in November 1912 to have a Sam Davis memorial window installed in the Museum of the Confederacy in Richmond. These monuments—probably the most prominent signs of Civil War heritage that Tennessee has yet produced—testified to the social power of the communities that produced them. Cunningham and his associates provide just one example of the ways in which middle-class whites across the South moved at the turn of the century to reclaim the space of historical memory and refurbish an image of southern whiteness. It was a cultural space in which class and gender differences were subsumed under a strict racial segregation and where commentators mitigated anxieties about the New South by alluding to a comforting, mythical past.

Sumner Cunningham died on December 20, 1913, but his efforts live on. Cunningham had done more than erect a monument on the State Capitol to Sam Davis—the only other Tennessean after Andrew Jackson to be so honored. The Sam Davis cult has outlived by decades its principal architect, and although his ambition to enshrine Davis in the pantheon of American heroes was not fully realized, the memorialization of Davis in Tennessee has remained strong. Cunningham facilitated a folk history that permeated regional memories of the Civil War. In this exercise he was not alone; the Sam Davis story has been sustained and promoted by some of the leading figures of historical memory in Tennessee. In 1928 folklorist and Tennessee state librarian John Trotwood Moore, a Klan supporter and incorrigible racist, was asked to write a few lines for a promotional brochure launching the new "Sam Davis Hotel" in downtown Nashville. He started to draft the story with these lines: "This boy's martyrdom has no equal in all the annals of war. Many have given their lives for their country or their friends, but Sam Davis gave his rather than break his word to . . ." Moore trailed off at this point, however, perhaps mindful of the hyperbole or perhaps thinking that to complete the thought—"rather than break his word to *the enemy*"—was too bold a recollection of Civil War enmities for a commercial brochure. Moore had expressed this view before. In an earlier poem to Davis, he had concluded with the lines "*For Martyr of all martyrs he / Who dies to save an enemy!*"—a reference to the supposed fact that Davis's informer was in the Union army. Scratching these thoughts, Moore proceeded in the hotel brochure with a straight description of a story from the written testimonials that he had collected as custodian of the state archives. He could not resist adding a few embellishments of his own, though, and depicted a gallows scene in which Davis, noose around his neck, was again offered "his horse, his side-arms and a free pass" if only he would reveal his informer. The state librarian penned Sam Davis's last words as "I am ready. Do your duty, men."[21]

These thoughts came a year after the State of Tennessee formally adopted the Sam Davis story and began to fund its promotion as official state history. In 1927, after years of lobbying by the UDC, the State purchased the Davis family home in Smyrna, granting the request of the Sam Davis Memorial Association to appropriate funds for the site. The association's charter of incorporation made explicit its aim "to beautify, preserve and adorn the [home] throughout all coming years in a manner most befitting the memory of that great soldier and hero, and commensurate with the gratitude of his countrymen; and to acquire, own and display all historic or literary productions, relics, mementoes relating to, and otherwise memorializing his life and character." During the 1930s the association converted the home and its adjoining 168 acres into a veritable shrine to a mythical antebellum South, conveying, in the words of its promotional literature, "a heartening atmosphere of simplicity, sincerity, and an enduring timelessness of a fine way of life." Three generations of custodians have carefully cultivated this image—planting cotton, oats, and barley in the fields, maintaining fences and outbuildings, and even restoring slave cabins (transferred from a neighboring plantation site). Today, you can even get married at the Sam Davis home. Apparently some couples see no irony in tying the knot at a shrine to a lost cause.[22]

Although the "big house," lovingly restored and tendered, has served as the grand stage for the Sam Davis story, little effort has been given until recently to establishing the authenticity of African American life on the Davis plantation. The cabins, like the old smokehouse, have stood as empty stage props to the main museum. This studied silence about slavery strongly contrasts with the memorial association's wide-ranging efforts over many years to sustain Sam Davis's story in the collective memory of Tennesseans, particularly its efforts to encourage school children to visit the shrine. In 1940, for example, the association wrote to each member of the Tennessee State Board of Education "asking to have a Sam Davis Day in the public schools." In 1946 the association sent a copy of a biography of Davis to each school in Middle Tennessee and regularly encouraged schoolteachers to bring their young scholars, white and black, to the home. Other mechanisms used by the association to sustain Davis's memory in the public imagination include annual picnics, commemoration and dedication services, and occasional feature articles in regional periodicals—including the *Tennessee Historical Quarterly*. During the Civil War Centennial observances in the early 1960s, the board of trustees wrote to the Postmaster General of the United States requesting the issuance of a stamp in honor of Sam Davis. The request was politely tabled.[23]

After World War II, with veterans again enjoying the respect of a grateful people, the State of Tennessee stepped up its support of the Sam Davis story and in 1947 appropriated $15,000 for an additional statue at the site of the execution in

The commemoration of the Confederate martyr continued in the decades following Cunningham's 1913 death. In 1927, the state of Tennessee purchased the Davis family home as a memorial site, and the following year saw the opening of Nashville's Sam Davis Hotel, pictured here in a postcard produced by Curteich-Chicago.

Pulaski. The state assembly appropriated an additional $6,000 for improvements to the Sam Davis Home. This was on top of the home's annual appropriation of $4,000 and meant that, next to a program setting historical markers on the state's highways, efforts to commemorate Davis received more state funding that year than any other historical project. In making these allocations, state legislators were confirming that the ideal veteran for the Volunteer State was a white, male Confederate; World War II African American veterans could have had no expectation of a similar effort to correlate their service with that of the thousands of Tennessee African Americans who served in the Union army during the Civil War. Speaking at the dedication of the execution-site statue in 1951, Tennessee State Librarian and Archivist Dan M. Robison justified these expenditures in terms that again underscored the invisible yet central white racial identity at the heart of the state's actions: "True it is that thousands of other young men gave their lives in that tragic War Between the States, and still other thousands have gallantly met death in the wars that preceeded [sic] and followed that conflict. But because of his behaviour [sic] here in Pulaski, Sam Davis has become to all of us the symbol of modest and steadfast courage, devotion to duty and country, and of good faith to those who put their trust in him."[24]

Robison's remarks suggest that by the early 1950s Davis had become the quintessential representative of gallantry and honor in the ordinary soldier. But in stressing that Davis's "behaviour here in Pulaski" had become "to all of us" symbols of honor and patriotism, Robison indulged in a biased interpretation of the event. True enough, Union soldiers had admired the condemned soldier's fortitude and bravery in the face of death — a northern eyewitness correspondent described him as "gifted" and "fearless" — but they also judged Davis deserving of death because of his "wicked" actions and described the prisoner's demeanor as "indignant" and "scornful." Nonetheless, Robison proceeded to portray Davis as an American hero, comparing him to the Cold War intelligence operators working behind enemy lines in Russia. "While we pay tribute here to one who was hanged as a spy in the long ago," he said, "may we not think with gratitude of those men and women who today serve their country in so dangerous and thankless a way." In Robison's eulogy, then, was another effort to neutralize the circumstances of the execution and to refurbish Davis as an all–American hero. His remarks can also be read as an exercise in making the "whiteness" of the commemoration virtually invisible. The "all of us" signified an appeal to a particular community in the Jim Crow crowd gathered off the court square in Pulaski — white Tennesseans of a Confederate heritage or sympathy. "We Southerners insist that Sam Davis was a scout and not a spy, and there is good ground for that contention," Robison continued, but he had little more to say on the matter of the Lost Cause. By such sleight of hand Robison claimed as national memory the story of a servant of a white supremacist move to secede from the United States to protect and preserve the institution of slavery.[25]

The racial politics of remembrance can be seen more clearly in remarks made by commemorative speakers at the Sam Davis Memorial Association's annual membership meeting. Invited speakers from the 1950s and 1960s included former governors, church ministers, and senior educators from the region's universities. In June 1961, as the nation's Civil War centennial celebrations began, Herman Norton, acting dean of Vanderbilt University's school of religion, lauded Davis's courage, discipline, and dedication — values he claimed were required in our time as "we ourselves are being tested . . . to meet the needs of our day." Norton spoke at a time of heightened international tensions associated with the Cold War and when sit-ins and other civil rights protests had destabilized the racial status quo in Middle Tennessee.

The previous year's speaker, Jesse Burt, a Vanderbilt graduate, was more ex-

Educational programs run by the Sam Davis home (here) offer the possibility, at least, for more balanced portrayals of the Civil War and its legacy. Photograph courtesy of the Rutherford County Convention and Visitors Bureau.

plicit in using a Civil War context for Davis to animate the racial politics of the day. Noting that the United States stood alone as "an unwilling goal of the aggressive force known as Communism," Burt pointed to domestic disturbances as evidence of the "irresponsibility so prevalent in our own free society," warning that "the seeds of communism are . . . planted in fertile areas of unrest, dissension, and strife." Here Burt referred to the Nashville sit-in movement and the furor caused by Vanderbilt's expulsion of one of its leaders, African American divinity-school student James Lawson, which led to the resignations of nine professors from the divinity school and widespread bad press for the university. Speaking at the Sam Davis home a week after the events, Burt condemned the actions of civil rights activists, describing their actions as "rigged sit-ins," adding that youth was no excuse for such irresponsible actions. "Sam Davis was young too," he said, and though "the Communists say that history and heroes aren't important," we "do well to pay him homage, learning from him, being inspired by him." Burt was of course missing a delicious irony: he criticized pacifist civil rights radicalism as anti–American by honoring a man who had taken up arms in open rebellion against the United States. It seems clear that he used this memory of Sam Davis to validate a social system based on racial segregation and undercut challenges to that system.[26]

"All Tennesseans know the story of Sam Davis," noted three historians in a short history of Tennessee published for college use in the 1960s. While memories of Davis are an indelible part of regional memory, the story did not take a firm hold outside of Tennessee in spite of occasional efforts after World War II to give the story a wider currency. In the 1950s a theatrical production of the "Sam Davis Story" played to packed audiences in Nashville's Ryman Auditorium and became the basis of a radio drama, "Honor Bound," broadcast to U.S. troops overseas. In January 1961 noted Civil War historian Bruce Catton included Davis's story in an illustrated article titled "Gallant Men in Deeds of Glory" in *Life* magazine. "For as long as southern memory endures," Catton noted, "the name of Sam Davis will stand for unflinching loyalty." In the late 1940s or early 1950s, Illustrated Features Syndicate produced a cartoon strip called "The Story of Sam Davis" for newspaper circulation. In this guise, Davis, looking remarkably like Clark Gable, is depicted as an all–American hero caught up in a tragic era. Despite the occasional cultural performance of Davis's memory outside Tennessee, the evidence does not suggest that his story has traveled into the collective consciousness of Americans as a latter-day Nathan Hale of the Civil War.[27]

In the post-civil rights era, Tennesseans have continued to honor Davis, who in 1992 was named "Historical Personality of the Year" by the Tennessee Historical Commission. His shrine persists for many as a mythic idyll of white antebellum society and as the cradle of a pure and heroic character. Yet the story of Sam Davis, while strong and immutable for some, has been challenged in recent years by the progressive and professional views of others. In the early 1990s, historical preservationists at Middle Tennessee State University (MTSU) recognized the interpretive potential of the home as a historic site. They criticized the "shrine mentality" and the lack of authenticity in the material culture and historical interpretation of the site. "The Sam Davis Home," argued Andrew Gulliford, director of the Public History and Historical Preservation Program at MTSU, "is one of the few historic houses in the state that still has enough land around it to offer excellent opportunities to actually step back into the past and experience history." The custodians of the Confederate flame, however, complained bitterly about policy changes that were "inconsistent with the original purpose" of the home. The flying of the U.S. flag was, the Nashville chapter of the UDC charged, "an insult, not only to Sam Davis and his family, but to the entire Confederacy and its descendants."

The complainants were also unhappy with the renewed focus upon historical preservation. The site was established as "a Confederate shrine," they argued, "and we believe that original purpose has been lost in the shuffle." The symbols of the Confederacy "should not be hidden away in a closet," they concluded, "while the enemy flag flies, nor its lessons ignored in favor of a demonstration of corn planting or basket weaving." In the summer and fall of 1992, the SDMA was barraged with letters and telephone calls from Confederate supporters angered by the rumor that the battle flag of the Confederacy no longer flew at the Sam Davis Home. Malcolm Patton, regent of the association, was moved to write in the *Dixie Liberator* that the concerns were "misplaced." "The only trouble we have is trying to satisfy different demands over which Confederate flag should be flown on a regular basis. At the present time, in an attempt to please as many of our supporters as possible, the several Confederate flags are flown on a rotating basis; but a Confederate flag is always flown." The conflict between the Confederate memorialists and the historical preservationists led to a fight over changes to the bylaws and the constitution of the association's board of trustees. The preservationists, including Gulliford, were eventually maneuvered out as trustees in 1995. The effect of this could be seen in the coverage given to African Americans at the Sam Davis Home in the late 1990s and early 2000s. When I visited the home during that time, two slave cabins—which had been moved from a Polk family plantation, "Rattle & Snap," fifty miles south of Nashville—were filled with farm implements and bore a sign reporting that Charles Davis (Sam's father) had owned fifty-one slaves in 1860, making him the fourth largest slaveholder in the district. The notice concluded with these words: "Only a few of their names are known and nothing else is known about them"—period.[28]

Most recently, however, ambivalence about the meaning of the Sam Davis Home has begun to reshape the ground on which it stands. During black history month in 2001, a temporary exhibit in one of the slave cabins explored the African origins of slave music culture. More recently, with the support of a new director at the Sam Davis Home, scholars from the sociology and anthropology departments at MTSU excavated the remains of the fourteen residences that housed over fifty enslaved African Americans from 1850 to 1865. More than fifteen thousand artifacts were recovered during the five-week dig, and these are currently being catalogued and a report prepared for publication. A temporary exhibition during the winter of 2005–06 presents some of the archaeological data. "As time proceeds and more of the needed documentary research is completed," remarked project director Kevin E. Smith, "we will hope to transform parts of the temporary exhibit into the permanent exhibit space on the slaves who lived at the Charles Davis Farm." Complimenting this work, the Sam Davis Home now runs educational outreach programs focusing on the material culture of the mid-nineteenth century, civil war medicine, the music of slaves, and the lives of soldiers and civilians during the Civil War.[29]

These developments point towards the possibility of new ways of interpreting the South's relationship to its Confederate past and the decades of memorialization of the Lost Cause that followed. It seems possible that the Sam Davis Home could become a site for both black and white historical narratives, commemorating not only the life of a valiant young soldier and his family but also the stories of the many southerners and their families enslaved on the farm. Mapping and representing the complexities of the region's nineteenth-century history will require brave and resilient leadership from the State of Tennessee, the officers of the s d m a, academics at the local universities, and other community groups. It will also require the defeat of those who see the story of Sam Davis as grounded in an immutable historical identity that denies the histories of others. The Sam Davis story, as developed in the 1890s by Sumner Cunningham, was not a conscious effort to falsify history but an attempt to meet a particular need at a unique time in a society's history. In commemorating Sam Davis, however, Cunningham and others disparaged other voices, other lives. As southern society evolves, its symbols, myths, and stories must evolve as well.

The weight of past memorialization, however, cannot be underestimated. Today the vast archive of social memory centered on one Confederate soldier is as yet unchallenged by a single monument in any county seat to the 20,133 African Americans who served in Tennessee's colored Union regiments. "One can still see statues and parks in Tennessee in honor of Forrest, but none to black soldiers," historian Bobby L. Lovett remarked in 1976 — and this situation persists even as we approach the 150th anniversary of the war. Given that almost 40 percent of black males aged eighteen to forty-five years in Middle Tennessee were serving in the Union army by 1865, we could assume that several of the fifty-one slaves on Charles Davis's farm in 1860 must have enlisted in the Union army. Recovering their stories will not be easy, but it is vital if the South is to recover its true past.[30]

NOTES

Earlier versions of this essay were presented in 2001 at the annual meetings of the American Popular Culture Association in Philadelphia and at the British Association of American Studies. I am grateful for the comments received on those occasions. Paul Davis Murfree's interest in the Sam Davis story during a course I taught at Vanderbilt University on "The Civil War and Reconstruction in American Memory" was a catalyst for the development of this paper. I am grateful to Davis (a distant relative of Sam Davis) for many stimulating conversations about the story's significance, which he explored in his seminar paper, "A Hero Emerges." Thanks also to Don H. Doyle, Larry J. Griffin, Samuel T. McSeveney, and David S. Karr — as well as the anonymous reviewers of this journal — for comments on earlier drafts.

1. Program, Confederate Memorial Service, 2 June 2001, hosted by General Joseph E. Johnston Camp No. 28, Sons of Confederate Veterans, Nashville, Tennessee, copy in author's possession; "Monument's Placement Upsets Some," *Tennessean*, 21 July 1999.

2. See Martha E. Kinney, "If Vanquished I am Still Victorious: Religious and Cultural Symbolism in Virginia's Confederate Memorial Day Celebrations, 1866–1930," *Virginia Magazine of History & Biography* 106 (Summer 1998): 237–67. The most influential theoretical exposition of collective memory is Maurice Halbwachs, *On Collective Memory*, ed., trans., and intro. Lewis A. Coser (1941; rprt. University of Chicago Press, 1992). See also the excellent collection of essays in John R. Gillis, ed., *Commemorations: The Politics of National Identity* (Princeton University Press, 1994). For an application of Halbwachs's theoretical approach to the Civil War era, see David W. Blight's "For Something beyond the Battlefield: Frederick Douglass and the Struggle for the Memory of

the Civil War," *Journal of American History* 75 (March 1989): 1156–78. For application to southern history, see W. Fitzhugh Brundage, ed., *Where These Memories Grow: History, Memory, and Southern Identity* (University of North Carolina Press, 2000).

3. See franklin forts, "Living with Confederate Symbols," *Southern Cultures* (Spring 2002): 60–75; David W. Blight, "Quarrel Forgotten or a Revolution Remembered? Reunion and Race in the Memory of the Civil War, 1875–1913," in Blight and Brooks D. Simpson, eds., *Union & Emancipation: Essays on Politics and Race in the Civil War Era* (Kent State University Press, 1997), 160.

4. "The Execution of a Rebel Spy," Cincinnati *Daily Commercial*, 8 December 1863. None of the previous commentators on the execution of Sam Davis appear to have been aware of this source.

5. Events surrounding the execution have become the stuff of legend—but during the course of my research I was surprised to find that many of the descriptive features of the popular legend of Sam Davis's execution are well-grounded in primary sources. This account was reconstructed from the papers of the military trial, from the journalist's report in the Cincinnati *Daily Commercial*, 8 December 1863, and from four accounts written at various times by Union soldiers who witnessed the hanging: J. C. Harwood Diary, 1863–1864, 1 vol. mf 9, Tennessee State Library and Archives (hereinafter, TSLA); Captain H. I. Smith, "Union Veteran's Tribute to Davis," *Confederate Veteran* (hereinafter *CV*) 3 (December 1895): 373; "Letter from Gen. Dodge," *CV* 5 (July 1897): 355–58; "The Sam Davis Overcoat," *CV* 5 (July 1897): 358–59. Of the many secondary-source accounts of the execution, I have found the following to be the most reliable—or at least the clearest on primary source citations: John Bakeless, *Spies of the Confederacy* (1970; rprt. Dover Publications, 1997), 205–42. Many sources cite a story of the execution that appeared in a Federal army publication, the *Pulaski Chanticleer*, 2 December 1963.

6. The best accounts of Middle Tennessee during the war years can be found in Stephen V. Ash, *Middle Tennessee Society Transformed, 1860–1870: War and Peace in the Upper South* (Louisiana State University Press, 1988); Stephen V. Ash, *When the Yankees Came: Conflict and Chaos in the Occupied South, 1861–1865* (University of North Carolina Press, 1995); Fremantle made the observation at Wartrace, Tennessee, on June 1, 1863. Walter Lord, ed., *The Fremantle Diary: Being the Journal of Lieutenant Colonel James Arthur Lyon Fremantle, Coldstream Guards, and his Three Months in the Southern States* (Little, Brown, 1954), 126; see the Provost Marshall files on microfilm at the TSLA. I am grateful to Dr. Michael Bradley of Motlow State Community College for informing me of the evidence of executions described within this source; Nashville *Daily Union*, 16 May and 10 June 1863; "Train Ride from Chattanooga to Nashville," Boston *Evening Transcript*, 21 January 1864.

7. See "Children's Corner—Top 12 Artifacts," http://www.tnmuseum.org/children/artifacts.html (accessed 7 February 2003). The four biographies are S. A. Cunningham, *Sam Davis, the Story of an Old-Fashioned Boy* (Confederate Veteran, 1914); Edythe J. R. Whitley, *Sam Davis, Confederate Hero, 1842–1863* (Sam Davis Memorial Association, 1947); Mabel Goode Frantz, *Full Many a Name: The Story of Sam Davis, Scout and Spy, C. S. A.* (McCowat-Mercer Press, Inc., 1961); Beverly A. Rude, *Sam: The Civil War Experiences of Private Samuel Davis* (Tacitus Publications, 1993). See also two notable collections of materials on Sam Davis housed in the TSLA: "Sam Davis," Civil War Collection: Confederate and Federal, 1861–1865, box 15, folder 8, and "Sam Davis," John Trotwood Moore Papers, box 30, folder 3.

8. Sam R. Watkins, *"Co. Aytch": A Side Show of the Big Show* (1882; rprt. Simon & Schuster, 1990), 95. J. B. Killebrew's piece, originally published in the *Nashville Union and American*, 30 June and 4 July 1871, was reprinted in the *Annals of the Army of Tennessee* (1878) and *Military Annals of Tennnessee* (1883); *Giles County: History of Franklin, Giles, Lincoln, and Moore Counties, Tennessee* (Good-

speed Publishing Company), 749–66, copy accessed on-line at http://www.tngenweb.org/giles/history/gs.html (accessed 7 February 2003).

9. C. Vann Woodward quoted in Nina Silber, *The Romance of Reunion: Northerners and the South, 1865–1990* (University of North Carolina Press, 1993), 4; Allen Tate, *Memories and Essays Old and New 1926–1974* (Carcanet Press, 1976), 146.

10. *CV* 1 (January 1893): 1; S. A. Cunningham, "Sam Davis," *American Historical Magazine* 4 (July 1899): 195.

11. "A Union Soldier's Tribute," *CV* 3 (May 1895): 149.

12. "In Memory of Samuel Davis," *CV* 3 (May 1895), 149; "About a Monument to Samuel Davis," *CV* 3 (September 1895): 258.

13. Simpson, *Cunningham*, 147; "How Shall Samuel Davis Be Honored," *CV* 3 (August 1895): 240. Charles Reagan Wilson persuasively describes the use of Christian imagery in the development of a "civil religion" among Lost Cause enthusiasts—see his *Baptized in Blood: The Religion of the Lost Cause, 1865–1920* (University of Georgia Press, 1980). "November 27—Anniversaries," *CV* 3 (November 1895): 336–37.

14. "Federal Veterans at Shiloh," *CV* 3 (April 1895): 104–5. See also the useful account of Cunningham's role in promoting the Sam Davis myth in John A. Simpson, *S. A. Cunningham and the Confederate Heritage* (University of Georgia Press, 1994), 146–49. Grace Hale, *Making Whiteness: The Culture of Segregation in the South, 1890–1940* (Vintage, 1998), 9.

15. For commemoration of Forrest, see Court Carney, "The Contested Image of Nathan Bedford Forrest," *Journal of Southern History* 67 (August 2001): 601–31. For an example of the debate over public school textbooks, see the debate between Garrett and an East Tennessean critic in W. R. Garrett, "Controverted Points in Tennessee History," *American Historical Magazine* 6 (1901): 118–73.

16. Varina Davis quoted in John A. Simpson, "S. A. Cunningham and the Confederate Heritage," PhD dissertation, University of Oregon, 1987, 495, emphasis added; *CV* 3 (December 1895): 370; 4 (May 1896): 143; 8 (March 1900): 100; "Union Veteran's Tribute to Davis," *CV* 3 (December 1895): 373; "Letter from Gen. Dodge," *CV* 5 (July 1897): 355–58. A copy of the military tribunal transcript is held in the Civil War Collection—Confederate, box 15, folder 8, "Sam Davis," TSLA; "The Sam Davis Overcoat," *CV* 5 (July 1897): 358–59.

17. These activities are described in Simpson, "S. A. Cunningham," 348–51; see also "The Drama 'Sam Davis'," *CV* 4 (October 1896): 399; "The Sam Davis Drama," *CV* 4 (November 1896): 402; "Game of Confederate Heroes," *CV* 6 (July 1898): 304; Herman Justi, ed., *Official History of the Tennessee Centennial Exposition* (1898), 133–34.

18. Quoted in Cunningham, "Sam Davis," 205–6.

19. Sally (Lawing) Ivie scrapbooks, vol. 3, Tennessee Historical Society Collection, TSLA.

20. Copies of correspondence relating to the Sam Davis Monument Committee can be found in the Clarkson Family papers, X-M-6 ac. no. 90–258, TSLA; "A Son of the Old South," Nashville *Tennessean*, 30 April 1909.

21. J. W. Pritchett to John Trotwood Moore, 5 January 1928 [with attachments], in John Trotwood Moore Papers, box 30, folder 3, TSLA. For evidence of Moore's solicitation of material and stories pertaining to Sam Davis, see J. L. Voorhies to Moore, 8 March 1923, and Moore to Henderson Yokely, 12 March 1923, in "Sam Davis," Confederate Collection, box 15, folder 8, TSLA.

22. 23 May 1930, Minutes, Sam Davis Memorial Association Records (SDMAR); Charter of incorporation dated 23 April 1930, quoted in Andrew Gulliford to Devereaux Cannon, 14 May 1993, box 1, Gulliford Collection, Middle Tennessee State University (MTSU); box 2, file 2, SDMAR.

23. Box 1, file 1, p.159, SDMAR; 19 June 1946, box 1, folder 4, Minutes Book 1, 3 June–2 August 1946. See also 3 June 1955 minutes, box 2, folder 3, Minutes Book VII, 6 September 1951–3 June 1955, SDMAR; Mary Gramling Braly, "If I Had a Thousand Lives—," *Tennessee Historical Magazine* 11 (July 1931): 261–69; Owen Nichols Meredith, "The Sam Davis Home," *Tennessee Historical Quarterly* 24 (Winter 1965); Frank C. Armstrong Jr. to Mrs. H. F. Ambrose, 16 March 1960, box 2, SDMAR.

24. 76th General Assembly, *Public Acts of Tennessee* (1947), sec. 5, item 41, p. 989, quoted in Dan M. Robison, personal papers, State Librarian and Archivist Papers, RG 34, ser. 13, box 74, folder 12, "Dedication of Sam Davis Memorial, Pulaski, Tennessee," TSLA; Dan M. Robison, "Remarks to be Delivered at the Dedication of the Sam Davis Memorial, Pulaski, Tennessee, November 27, 1950," State Librarian and Archivist Papers, box 74, folder 12, TSLA, quotation from p. 4.

25. Cincinnati *Daily Commercial*, 8 December 1863; Robison, "Remarks," quotations from pp. 6 & 7.

26. 8 June 1961, box 2, folder 6, book X, Minutes March, 1960–July 1961, SDMAR; "The Legacy of Sam Davis of Tennessee," address by Dr. Jesse C. Burt Jr. to the Sam Davis Memorial Association, 9 June 1960, box 2, SDMAR. A good account of the Nashville sit-ins and Lawson's expulsion from Vanderbilt University is Paul K. Conkin, *Gone with the Ivy: A Biography of Vanderbilt University* (University of Tennessee Press, 1985), 547–80.

27. Stanley J. Folmsbee, Robert E. Corlew, and Enoch L. Mitchell, *Tennessee: A Short History* (University of Tennessee Press, 1969), 340; Wilson, *Baptized in Blood*, 53; Bruce Catton, "Gallant Men in Deeds of Glory," *Life* Magazine, 6 January 1961. The other heroes depicted by Catton include a number of Confederates—Major John Pelham (the "Gallant Cannoneer"), Lieutenant John Singleton Mosby ("The Impudent Raider"), and Sergeant Richard Kirkland ("A Dauntless Samaritan"). Illustrated Features Syndicate, "The Story of Sam Davis," Clarkson Papers, box 1, folder 11, TSLA. Davis fails to appear in recent general histories of the war and the Confederacy—see, for example, James M. McPherson, *Battle Cry of Freedom* (Oxford University Press, 1988), and Emory Thomas, *The Confederate Nation* (Harper & Row, 1979). A brief mention of Sam Davis, however, does appear in Ken Burns's 1990 PBS documentary series on the Civil War.

28. "Sam Davis Home Position Statement," addendum by Andrew Gulliford, 18 October 1991, box 1, folder 2, Gulliford Collection, Albert Gore Research Center, MTSU; United Daughters of the Confederacy Nashville Chapter Number One to Mrs Edwin P. Pool, Treasurer, Tennessee Division UDC, 14 January 1992, box 1, folder 5, Gulliford Collection, Albert Gore Research Center, MTSU; Malcolm Patton, "The Confederate Flag Flies at the Sam Davis Home," *Dixie Liberator* (Fall 1992): 10; R. Jan Jennings to Governor of the State of Tennessee, 17 July 1995, box 1, folder 1, Gulliford Collection, Albert Gore Research Center, MTSU; 1860 Slave Census, State of Tennessee (1860 Agricultural Census quoted in Rude, *Sam*, 5).

29. "Exhibit shows growth of slave music," Nashville *Tennessean*, 12 January 2001; private communication between the author and Professor Kevin E. Smith, 5 September 2005. The daily journal of the 2004 excavation can be found on-line at: http://www.mtsu.edu/~soc/SamDavis/index.html (accessed 5 September 2005).

30. Ira Berlin, ed., *Freedom: A Documentary History of Emancipation, 1861–67*, vol. 5 (Cambridge University Press, 1982), Table 1; Bobby L. Lovett, "The Negro's Civil War in Tennessee, 1861–1865," *Journal of Negro History* 61 (January 1976): 36–50, quotation from page 37. For a recent effort to rediscover the role played by African American soldiers from the rural counties of the Middle Tennessee heartland, see my remarks to the Maury County African American Historical Council, 16 March 2002, published as "Freedom's Soldiers: What Do We Know about the Black Civil War Soldiers of Maury County?" by Edward Harcourt, *Historic Maury* 38 (June 2002): 58–71.

Jim Crow's Drug War
Race, Coca Cola, and the Southern Origins of Drug Prohibition

by Michael M. Cohen

The story of the origins and early years of Coca-Cola — which contained small quantities of coca extracts until 1903 — helps illuminate changing southern and national perceptions of appropriate drug use. 1890s advertisement, courtesy of the Collections of the Library of Congress.

*A*t the end of the nineteenth century, the U.S. hunger for narcotics and cocaine was so notorious that one leading public-health official declared, "We are the drug-habit nation."[1] Today, Americans lustfully—if schizophrenically—consume huge quantities of both the illegal "dope" of stoners and street junkies and the equally profitable products of high-tech bioresearch labs and multinational pharmaceutical corporations. We are now, as we were a century ago, a people torn between, as the TV says, "just say no" and "the miracle of medicine." But what do we mean by "drugs"? The public imagination struggles mightily to preserve stark distinctions between the various kinds of "drugs": heroin, cocaine, cannabis, alcohol, anabolic steroids, nicotine, caffeine, aspirin, Ritalin, Viagra, Prozac, and OxyContin, to name but a dozen. The history of drug prohibition, however, shows us that the difference between a "poison" and a "medicine," between drugs as scourge or salvation, is not so easily determined. Are those who become dependent upon drugs victims of a physical disease, or are they criminals and moral deviants? When do personal, medical, or recreational decisions become a social menace? And is it the chemistry or the social status of the consumer that shapes these attitudes? After more than a century of the "war on drugs," the historical transformation of drug use in the United States between the 1890s and 1930s from the free and largely unknowing use of any drug to the strict regulation and criminalization of narcotics, cocaine, and cannabis remains largely misunderstood by the public.

At the root of the drug-prohibition movement in the United States is race, the driving force behind the first laws criminalizing drug use, which first appeared as early as the 1870s. In an era in which African Americans, Asian and Mexican immigrants, as well as most European immigrants—Jews, Slavs, and Catholic Irish and Italians—were considered racial others, white racial fears amplified the sense of public menace posed by drugs and drug users. The belief of Gilded Age whites that racial difference marked a biologically determined predisposition to, say, deviousness, slovenliness, or lustfulness served to supercharge the hazards posed by Catholic inebriation, black intoxication, or Chinese addictions.[2] The pleasure of drug taking not only endangered Protestant morality, but the association of specific drug pleasures with individual racial groups raised the dire threat of miscegenation and urban disorder.

The nation's first drug laws had appeared in San Francisco in the 1870s, unsuccessfully prohibiting whites from patronizing opium dens in Chinatown lest some white woman should fall into the hands of the yellow peril. Indeed, the first bans on smoking opium only applied to whites, as race mixing and not the health of Chinese immigrants was at issue. Organized nativism, including the Ku Klux Klan, played a crucial role in pressing for federal alcohol prohibition in the 1910s, marking the 18th Amendment as a failed attempt by the waning WASP establishment to curtail the sinful pleasures of urban Catholics and the immigrant working classes. One of America's favorite recreational drugs, marijuana, was banned in the 1930s as a way of criminalizing the tens of thousands of Mexican migrant farm workers who entered the Southwest in search of work. These laws have remained persistently ineffective in curbing America's desire for intoxication and have instead served to demonize and outlaw entire populations.[3]

In the Jim Crow South, the dynamics of race, gender, and the growth of a mass consumer culture combined with the reformist impulses of the Progressive era to wage war on the "Negro cocaine fiend."[4] The changes in Coca-Cola in this time period illustrate this point. Marketed exclusively to middle class and professional whites, Coca-Cola contained a small quantity of coca extracts until 1903. When Coca-Cola was introduced, cocaine was championed by doctors and psychologists, including Sigmund Freud, as a medical marvel. In the 1890s, however, the medical opinion of cocaine began to sour as its savage addictive potential revealed itself, leaving manufacturers and medical reformers to call for new regulations and controls on the drug's distribution. Cocaine users themselves did not become criminals until urban police and civic leaders in the New South generated a moral panic over the casual use of cocaine among urban blacks, blaming everything from rape to urban riots on the drug's influence. By the dawn of the twentieth century, the South's fears of "Negro cocaine fiends" running amok trumped the drug's commercial profits and medical benefits. Southern cocaine prohibition eventually merged into a federal drive to regulate a range of narcotics and cocaine, representing a rare instance of southern leadership in Progressive reform and a spectacular example of how Jim Crow politics influenced the entire nation in a way that can still be felt in the "war on drugs."

These Progressive reform measures focused on a single aspect of the complex social problem of mass drug addiction; by scapegoating black cocaine users, reformers overlooked the far more deeply rooted problem of an epidemic of narcotics addiction among southern white women at this time. The voices of the sufferers—black and white, male and female—were silenced by the edicts of medical professionals, politicians, and police, thereby promoting authoritarian over medical solutions and moral severity over compassion. While the demonization of black cocaine users focused attention on the public pleasures of a small number of urban African Americans in places like Atlanta and New Orleans, such racially charged fears not only obscured the widespread opiate addiction among poor whites but effectively relegated to a tormented secrecy the sufferings of thousands of middle- and upper-class white women, who, like the fictional Mrs. Henry Lafayette Dubose in Harper Lee's *To Kill a Mockingbird* (1960), were the South's true face of drug addiction at the turn of the last century.

Mrs. Dubose is the cantankerous old lady who lives in the decaying house down the block from Atticus Finch and his children, Jem and Scout. She is supposedly

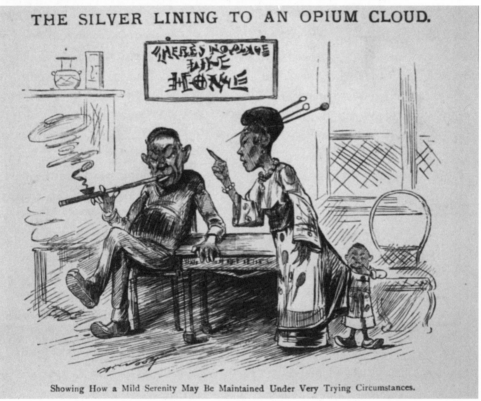

THE SILVER LINING TO AN OPIUM CLOUD.

THERE'S NO PLACE LIKE HOME

Showing How a Mild Serenity May Be Maintained Under Very Trying Circumstances.

The drug-prohibition movement in the United States took shape against the backdrop of racial anxieties—fears of African American "cocaine fiends," of "shifty" European immigrants, and of the stereotyped Chinese opium addict. Early-twentieth-century arrivals at Ellis Island being inspected for medical problems (above), and cartoon of a Chinese opium smoker (below), both courtesy of the Collections of the Library of Congress.

very sick, packs an old Confederate pistol, and yells at Jem and Scout as they pass her house on their way home from school. One day, the old lady shouts one insult too many, accusing their father of "lawin' for niggers," leading Jem to defend his father's honor by trampling Mrs. Dubose's flowerbeds. To make amends, Atticus sends the children to read Sir Walter Scott to Mrs. Dubose for two hours every day. These readings are quite painful for all involved. Mrs. Dubose passes the time either irritably ranting or wallowing in a delirium until an alarm clock announces the end of their reading session and her next dose of medicine. After a week, Atticus gathers the children to tell them that Mrs. Dubose died the previous evening. Strangely saddened by this news, the children ask their father why. "Mrs. Dubose was a morphine addict," explains Atticus. "She took it as a pain killer for years. The doctor put her on it. She'd have spent the rest of her life on it and died without so much agony, but she was too contrary. . . . She said she was going to leave this world beholden to nothing and nobody. . . . She was the bravest person I ever knew."[5]

This passing of a blameless and long-suffering southern drug addict presents us with a deeply sympathetic portrait of an uncompromising citizen of the Old South as it was gradually fading away. Mrs. Henry Lafayette Dubose richly embodies many of her generation's most iconic qualities: her proudly held aristocratic name (we never do learn her first name), widowed confinement within a decaying gothic mansion, phantom Confederate weapon, love of historical romance literature, unwavering commitment to white supremacy, and a closely guarded secret addiction to medically provided morphine. More than just another of Lee's colorful southern characters, Mrs. Dubose provides a very rare glimpse of what was a widespread, if carefully hidden, regional epidemic among southern white women at the turn of the last century. While it is difficult to determine precisely just how widespread drug addiction was at that time, David Courtwright, a historian of American drug use, has concluded that southern whites—and especially southern white women—probably had the highest rate of drug addiction of any population in the country, and perhaps the highest in the world.[6] Why was this the case?

For several years after the passage of the first comprehensive federal drug-control law, the Harrison Narcotic Act of 1914, a significant legal loophole permitted doctors and public health workers to establish "maintenance clinics" where drug addicts could receive legal prescriptions for heroin, morphine, and cocaine. An unusual and short-lived experiment in Progressive public-health reform, maintenance clinics operated under the assumption that drug addiction was a largely incurable, though treatable, *medical* condition. Guided by a desire to reduce the social harm of drug addiction—such as eliminating the crime caused by the addict's need for money to support a habit—these clinics provided prescription drugs and other health services to poor addicts, whatever their race, class, or sex, without prejudice. By studying the clinic records, public-health officials and historians discovered that drug addiction in cities across the South was, on average, a staggering 65 percent higher than in the urban centers of the North and West. Atlanta, Shreveport, Knoxville, Jacksonville, New Orleans, and Houston each outstripped cities like New Haven, New York, and Los Angeles in rates of addiction. The records of an innovative clinic opened in 1912 in Jacksonville, Florida, by Dr. Charles Terry revealed that out of the 646 addicts whose medical histories he studied closely, 416 were white (249 women and 167 men) while only 230 were black (131 women and 99 men). "Our population," Terry wrote, "is composed about equally of whites and colored so that it is seen that, with us at least, the whites are far more prone to drug addictions than the blacks." These clinic records also reveal a deep segregation in southern drug cultures: whites were overwhelmingly addicted to opiates whereas blacks tended to used cocaine. Terry also noted that elderly women addicts were found in large numbers and that "as the ages of users advance the proportion of females increase relatively." This racial and gender profile is repeated in clinic after clinic across the South. For example, the records from the State of Tennessee reveal that of the 2,370 drug addicts who registered with clinics in 1913, women comprised over two-thirds of the addicts and over 90 percent were white.[7]

There is a lot to question about these numbers. The clinics catered almost exclusively to poor and lower-class drug addicts who chose to seek the protection of medical help over a life of criminality and degradation. Due to the increasing public stigmatizing of drug addicts that began after 1900, rich white drug addicts like the fictional Mrs. Dubose could simply pay for a private doctor's prescriptions, the many mail-order cures, or the expensive, private rehabilitation hospitals that catered to these new demands.[8] Taking class distribution into account, the real demographic breakdown of drug addicts in the South should reveal far higher rates among white women than the clinic data alone suggest.

Wealthier drug addicts in the South—like Harper Lee's fictional Mrs. Dubose—could check themselves into such expensive rehabilitation clinics as the one advertised here in Medical World *in 1912.*

As the case of southern white women illustrates, the mass drug addiction of the late nineteenth century finds its source in the professional and commercial practice of medicine. Despite serious but spotty progress in the medical sciences, as late as the 1890s there was little to distinguish a legitimate doctor from a quack, and even less to distinguish a pharmacist from a snake-oil seller. "In no country in the world," wrote one outraged "doctor" in 1861, "is quackery carried on to so enormous an extent as it is in the United States."[9]

Even doctors who were genuinely concerned for their patient's health instead of just their own pocketbooks found very few tools in their medical bag capable of rendering real assistance to the suffering. Opiates, the most ancient substance in the human pharmacopoeia, were therefore very attractive medicines, for they were known to alleviate a range of symptoms for a few recognized diseases such as cholera. In addition, the legendary soporific qualities of opiates enabled doctors to treat their patients' pain and anxiety. The invention of the hypodermic syringe in 1853 accelerated the use of opiates. By the 1870s medical texts recommended the use of narcotics like morphine and laudanum to treat an ever broadening range of illnesses and behaviors, from consumption and insomnia to masturbation. As medical reliance grew into an overdependence upon narcotics, iatrogenic addiction—addiction induced unintentionally through the treatment of a physician—grew to epidemic proportions. Doctors spread addiction to their patients almost as quickly as they developed the habit themselves. This problem was so pervasive that in 1911 one Boston area physician estimated that "ten percent of the physicians of the United States are users of morphine through the hypodermic syringe," citing a "hospital where nearly all of the physicians and nurses use the drug." A 1912 poll of more than 150 physicians asked, "In your experience, what occupations have furnished the largest quota of drug habitues?" The breakdown of numbers was revealing: physicians (71), pharmacists (31), prostitutes (18), nurses (12) housewives (11), and unemployed (11).[10]

The presence of so many "housewives" on a list otherwise shared by medical professionals and the urban underworld suggests that wealthy white women suffered disproportionately from iatrogenic addiction because they had the greatest access to doctors. To make matters worse, physicians demonstrated little understanding of women's health, which led them to over-prescribe morphine for a long list of "women's illnesses," including menstrual cramps, labor and childbirth pains, menopausal symptoms, and a wide range of so-called "nervous illnesses." In the words of Mary Tyrone, Mrs. Dubose's fictional New England doppelganger and the neurasthenic, drug-addicted mother in Eugene O'Neill's *Long Day's Journey Into Night*, "I hate doctors! They'll do anything—anything to keep you coming to them. They'll sell their souls! What's worse, they'll sell yours, and you never know it till one day you find yourself in hell."[11]

In the South, the generally poor quality of health care exacerbated most of these sources of addiction. Until the 1920s southern doctors practiced what some called "states' rights medicine," which held that differences in climate and disease in the South demanded more dramatic doctoring with stronger drugs in higher doses. Doctors used large quantities of opiates to treat the symptoms of the trilogy of southern "lazy diseases"—malaria, hookworm, and pellagra—and persistent outbreaks of cholera and dysentery kept the use of opiates especially high. Some historians have pointed to the Civil War as a major source of addiction, and though these stories of victimized soldiers have been greatly exaggerated, drug addiction was known as the "soldier's disease" or the "army disease" for a generation after Appomattox. In the rural South, doctors worked more like traveling salesmen, distributing various drugs and a practiced bedside manner as they passed through small towns and hamlets. William Owens's memoir of growing up as a poor sharecropper in Pin Hook, Texas, gives us a glimpse of this amateurish quackery when his family desperately hires a traveling doctor to save his dying father:

> When there was nothing else to try, my mother sent for Dr. Reeves, a Pin Hook man who, after giving up as farmer, fiddler, dancing master, and preacher, had sent off for medical books and set himself up as a doctor. He lived on the north side of Pin Hook and kept his office and bottles and scales in a front room of his house.
>
> By the time Dr. Reeves came, my father could not raise himself in bed for the pain. . . .
>
> He took his bottles and balances from his saddlebags and put them on the table. He weighed out bits of white powders and mixed them on a paper with the blade of his pocket knife. With the blade he divided them into doses and raked them into envelopes. . . .
>
> "If these don't do any good, send me word. I've got some medicine at home that will."[12]

Owens's father died that day, but other patients who survived such haphazard pharmaceutical practices were often left addicted to the very medicines that cured them.

These very real medical dangers go a long way toward explaining why African Americans suffered from opiate addiction at far lower rates than southern whites. After Emancipation many southern doctors simply refused to treat African Americans, so while they were unjustly denied treatment, they did manage to escape iatrogenic addiction. The sheer poverty of southern African Americans also prevented them from hiring doctors and purchasing medicines in an era in which drug addiction was overwhelmingly a disease of the middle class and idle rich.[13]

For those who could not afford—or did not trust—doctors and quacks, there remained a serious danger of drug addiction from self-medication with patent medicines. Patent medicines were commercialized, prepackaged secret formulas and panaceas that claimed to cure just about anything from sexual dysfunction to cancer. Of course, patent medicines relied heavily on the same limited but effective medicine cabinet of opiates, cocaine, cannabis, and alcohol. One of the nation's most popular patent medicines, Mrs. Winslow's Soothing Syrup, was recommended for teething infants and contained morphine and alcohol as the two primary active ingredients. Another popular self-dosing catarrh remedy—used as a hay fever or asthma treatment—consisted simply of powdered cocaine.

The image of "medicine show" charlatans selling "snake oil" out of a wagon hardly does justice to the entrepreneurial spirit and industrial technology that most patent medicine manufacturers invested in their businesses. After the Civil War, the patent medicine industry became one of the most innovative branches of the rapidly expanding U.S. consumer economy. Because patent medicine manufacturers feared imitation and kept their ingredients secret, there was no real way to determine the quality, let alone the safety, of one bottle of medicine over another; consequently, manufacturers devised new forms of mass advertising to promote their products. Many of the strategies of modern advertising were first created by the patent medicine industry to hawk their little bottles of magic: branding and copyrighted logos, catchphrases and snazzy product names, celebrity endorsement and personal testimonials, as well as the direct appeal to a customer's personal anxiety, vanity, spiritual values, and sense of social status.[14]

Beyond simply consuming patent medicines, the New South proudly produced them in great quantities and varieties. The extremely popular PPP (Prickly Ash, Poke Root, and Potassium) was brewed in Savannah. Two former Union Army veterans moved to Chattanooga, where they bought up the patents for several antebellum formulas and made a fortune selling Black Draught and Wine of Cardui to a national market. Entrepreneurs in New Orleans manufactured Dr. Tichenor's Antiseptic Refrigerant, a topical anesthetic that was promoted "for cuts, bruises, sprains, superficial burns, sunburn and mouthwash" and carried the stars and bars of the Confederate flag on its label into drug stores nationwide. The capital of the New South, Atlanta also stood at the center of the region's patent-medicine industry, home to the nationally famous Ko-Ko Tulo's cure-all, Dr. Pierce's Pleasant Purgative Pellets, and BBB (Botanic Blood Balm). New South booster Henry Grady and Old South writer Joel Chandler Harris gave testimonial for the popular Atlanta-based Dr. Brigger's Huckleberry Cordial and Hunnicutts

DIRECTIONS FOR USING
DR. BIRNEY'S CATARRHAL POWDER.

This remedy contains two and one-half per cent of Cocaine and is prepared from a prescription of one of the foremost Nose and Throat specialists in the United States, and has been used in his practice for years with excellent success. As much care must be exercised in its use as is required in following the directions of your family physician.

HOW TO APPLY.

Insert the round end of glass tube into the powder, stirring it lightly about, as shown in Cut No. 1, until it contains about One-fourth inch of the powder. Then cover end of glass tube containing powder with rubber tubing, as shown in Cut No. 2. Then place flattened end of glass tube just within the nostril, as shown in cut. Then place the end of rubber tube between lips, inflate the cheeks and give a **short, quick puff**, and the powder will be diffused over the inner surface of the nose.

FOR CATARRH AND HAY FEVER.

Apply to both sides of the nostril morning and evening every other day for one week, then discontinue for one week. If not entirely relieved, repeat application as at first for one more week.

FOR CATARRHAL HEADACHE.

Apply to both sides of the nostril; if not entirely relieved, repeat application once more only in 30 minutes. If headache returns, apply same as for catarrh and hay fever.

FOR CATARRHAL DEAFNESS.

Apply to both sides of the nostril, same as for catarrh and hay fever.

You Blow The Powder.

TRADE MARK.

FOR ACUTE COLD IN HEAD.

Use the powder five or six times daily for one or two days; omit a day, then, if not relieved, repeat for one day more only.

FOR TONSILITIS, QUINSY AND SORE THROAT.

Have the powder blown over tonsils and throat by an assistant, the patient at the same time depressing the tongue with some flat instrument. Two OR THREE applications at intervals will suffice.

In ordinary cases of Nasal Catarrh, Hay Fever, Cold in the Head, Headache, Sore Throat, Tonsilitis and Quinsy, this Remedy will give immediate relief.

Patent medicines promised cures for just about every ailment. Mrs. Winslow's Soothing Syrup, for example, which was marketed as a way to relieve teething infants, contained morphine and alcohol. Cocaine was a common ingredient of many other remedies. Advertisements from the author's collection.

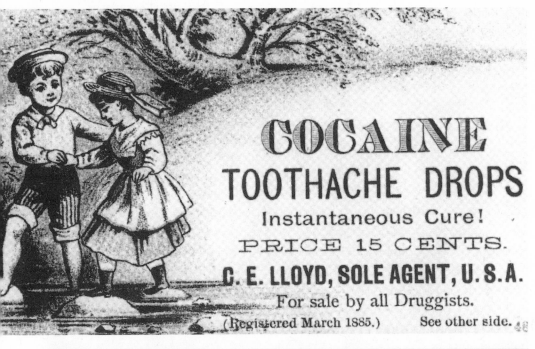

COCAINE
TOOTHACHE DROPS
Instantaneous Cure!
PRICE 15 CENTS.
C. E. LLOYD, SOLE AGENT, U.S.A.
For sale by all Druggists.
(Registered March 1885.)   See other side.

TEN REASONS WHY
COCARETTES
SHOULD BE USED BY ALL SMOKERS.

1st.—They are not injurious.

2d.—They are the most agreeable and pleasant "Smoke."

3d.—They are made of the finest Sun-cured Virginia Tobacco.

4th.—They have the exact proportion of genuine Bolivian Coca leaf combined with the finest flavored Tobacco, to produce the most delicious flavor.

5th.—The Coca neutralizes the depressing effects of the Nicotine in the tobacco.

6th.—Coca is the finest nerve tonic and exhilarator ever discovered.

7th.—Coca stimulates the brain to great activity and gives tone and vigor to the entire system.

8th.—Coca and Tobacco combined, is the greatest boon ever offered to smokers.

9th.—Cocarettes can be freely used by persons in delicate health without injury, and with positively beneficial results.

10th.—The Rice Paper used in wrapping Cocarettes is furnished by Messrs. May Brothers, New York, who are the American members of the celebrated French firm that for over 150 years have supplied the trade with this paper, the secret of making which was discovered by their ancestor Henry May. This paper, as now made by the house who conducts its enormous business under the style of "Compagnie Parisienne des Papiers a Cigarettes Francais," burns completely away, leaving no ashes whatever; it dies away in a thin vapor and the smoker inhales only the smoke of the Cocarette.

IMPORTANT
INFORMATION
FOR
SMOKERS

TRADE MARK

COCARETTES

MANF'D BY THE
COCABACCO CO.

SAINT   LOUIS

FAC-SIMILE OF WRAPPER

FOR SALE BY
ALL DEALERS

Rheumatic Cure. According to medical historian James Harvey Young, by 1890 Atlanta derived a higher proportion of its revenue from the patent-medicine industry than any other U.S. city.[15]

"THE REAL THING"

Of Atlanta's many patent medicines, none became as famous as the creation of a humble pharmacist named Dr. John Stith Pemberton, known the world over as the inventor of Coca-Cola. Born in 1831 near Knoxville, Georgia, Pemberton had an eclectic medical education, influenced equally by professional doctors and untrained herbalists. In 1855 he opened a drugstore in Columbus, Georgia, where he invented numerous medical concoctions, treated patients, and occasionally performed surgery. During the Civil War, Pemberton rose to the rank of Lieutenant Colonel in the Confederate Cavalry before suffering a serious injury in 1865, which began his life-long struggle with the "soldier's disease."[16]

In 1869 Pemberton followed thousands of ambitious southerners to Atlanta, where he hoped to make his fortune. Success eluded him until the early 1880s, when he fell in love with the newest wonder drug of the age, cocaine. After reading the glowing praise for the drug in British medical journals, he ordered a sample and began an extensive series of tests on himself. Claiming to have cured his own addiction to morphine, Pemberton declared cocaine a medical miracle, absolutely devoid of dangers and the singular solution to the growing middle-class disorder of "nervousness." Building off of the popularity of a French cocaine wine called Vin Mariani—a drink sold worldwide and promoted by three popes, Thomas Edison, and William McKinley—Pemberton invented his own knock-off French Coca Wine in 1884. One can glimpse Pemberton's chemically induced optimism and medicine-man sense of overstatement as he vigorously promoted his coca-wine to a select audience of white New South professionals:

Americans are the most nervous people in the world. . . . All who are suffering from any nervous complaints we commend to use that wonderful and delightful remedy, French Coca Wine, infallible in curing all who are afflicted with any nerve trouble, dyspepsia, mental and physical exhaustion, all chronic and wasting diseases, gastric irritability, constipation, sick headache, neuralgia, etc. . . . [C]lergymen, lawyers, literary men, merchants, bankers, ladies, and all whose sedentary employment causes nervous prostration, irregularities of the stomach, bowels and kidneys, who require a nerve tonic and a pure delightful diffusable stimulant, will find Coca Wine invaluable, a sure restorer to health and happiness. Coca is a most wonderful invigorator of the sexual organs and will cure seminal weakness, impotency, etc., when all other remedies fail.

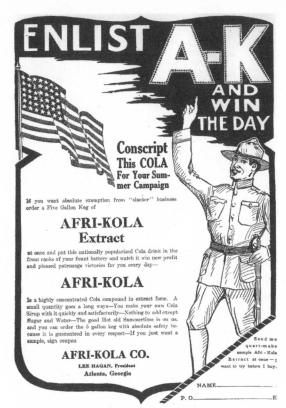

From the very start, Coca-Cola faced an array of competitors—from Koke and Pillsbury's Coke Extract to Afri-Kola. But somehow, everyone knew that Coca-Cola was "the real thing." Advertisement for Afri-Kola, from the author's collection.

Pemberton's promotion of cocaine as an aphrodisiac is worth emphasizing. As long as the consumption of coca-wine was directed at a white professional class, cocaine's sexual function appears healthy and energizing. But whatever its medicinal uses, Pemberton's French Coca Wine was a big success.

Unfortunately for Pemberton, this early success came at a bad time, for on November 25, 1885, the city of Atlanta voted to go completely dry for two years. Pemberton frantically set to work on a replacement, what he called a "temperance beverage," that could retain the medicinal effects that he desired from cocaine but without the alcohol. The resulting "soft drink" arrived in the spring of 1886. Explicitly named after Pemberton's two favorite ingredients, coca extract and the caffeine-rich extracts of the African Kola nut, the new Coca-Cola was strong stuff indeed.[17]

Celebrated as an "intellectual beverage and temperance drink," Coca-Cola was an immediate success in the highly fashionable soda fountains of Atlanta. Unlike the demonized saloons and bars, known for their working-class crowds, race-mixing, and unsavory women, soda fountains constituted a decidedly middle-class kind of urban social space. Known as the first place to serve Coca-Cola syrup with carbonated water, Joseph Jacobs's drug store in the center of Atlanta's

Five Points district instantly became the epicenter of the New South's consumer culture. Rigidly segregated by race and class, soda fountains attracted an affluent white patronage by appealing to women and children with healthy and respectable Coca-Cola mixed with soda water instead of alcohol.[18] Like any successful product, Coca-Cola soon spawned a large number of competing cocaine sodas: Dope Cola, Koca-Nola, Afri-Kola, Pillsbury's Coke Extract, Koke, Pau-Pau Cola, Cane Cola, Rococola, Wisola, and dozens more. Despite the competition, everybody knew that Coca-Cola was the real thing, and it quickly garnered the popular nickname of "dope"—then, as now, a generic term for a pleasurable drug. Coca-Cola successfully and explicitly blended state-of-the-art medical technology with middle-class consumer pleasure in a way previously unimagined.

Pemberton died in 1888 at the age of fifty-seven, his health weakened from two decades of addiction to morphine and cocaine. His business partner, Asa Grigs Candler, rose to become president and owner of the company. Never a reputable chemist in his own right, Candler specialized in promotion, writing advertising copy, and making deals. He moved his factory to Decatur Street, where he turned the "brain tonic" into one of the New South's largest export businesses, a proud southern monopoly to rival James Buchanan Duke's American Tobacco Company.

Just as Coca-Cola's sales took off in the summer of 1891, however, a telltale sign of future troubles appeared when the *Atlanta Constitution* started asking questions: "What's in Coca-Cola?" It was, and still is, a good question. The original formula for Coca-Cola was then, as now, shrouded in secrecy, but experienced consumers could taste the distinctive flavor of cocaine in the popular fountain drink. "I am told by a physician," reported an anonymous source in the *Constitution*'s article, "that the ingredient which makes coca cola so popular is cocaine. There is evidently enough of it in the drink to affect people and it is insidiously but surely getting thousands of people into the cocaine habit."[19]

Beyond simply attacking Coca-Cola, this article coincided with a much larger transformation of medical attitudes towards drugs. During the 1890s, the peak of drug consumption in U.S. history, scientific opinion rather rapidly turned against cocaine. Doctors who had once enthusiastically prescribed cocaine to cure narcotics addicts soon discovered that although cocaine freed their patients from morphine, this sickness simply transformed into an even more damaging addiction to cocaine. The growing professional animus towards cocaine marked a startling reversal, and in less than a decade cocaine took its place as the "third scourge of mankind," after alcohol and narcotics. It is important to understand, however, that surgeons and doctors did not abandon cocaine as an effective anesthetic and surgical tool. Nor did cocaine use immediately become a social crisis. Iatrogenic cocaine addicts during this moment of scientific transition donned the mantle of victimization, earning professional and popular sympathy rather than scorn.[20]

In its early decades, Coca-Cola was marketed as, among other things, an energy-boosting refreshment for the white middle-class—especially "Brain Workers" in search of a clear head. Advertisements from the author's collection.

As the most prominent national product containing the newly health-threatening substance, Coca-Cola came under fire from religious and civic leaders as a dangerous vice. Candler argued that there had to be a clear distinction between cocaine and the extract from the coca plant: one a dangerous menace, the other an enlivening tonic. (This is merely a question of concentration rather than substance, rather akin today to the difference between crack and powder cocaine.) Candler also took out an advertisement in the *Atlanta Constitution* confessing that the amount of coca in Coca-Cola was very small and that "no sensible person would undertake to say that this quantity [of coca] in a gallon would hurt a person taking a glass of the beverage."[21] Indeed, Candler had no intention of removing the cocaine from Coca-Cola. By changing the formula, he ran the risk of losing both his patent and his growing market share. As the tobacco industry knows best, addiction is a powerful method of maintaining consumer demand, and Candler's affluent customers had come to rely upon the tangy zip of Coca-Cola's secret ingredient in their soda-fountain favorite. Nevertheless, Candler sought to weather this first storm by downplaying Coca-Cola's medicinal benefits, and promoting the product's "refreshing" and "great tasting" qualities—a claim that most of the intentionally foul-tasting patent medicines could not make.

In 1899 an even greater controversy arose when Candler began selling Coca-Cola to a vastly expanded national market in distinctively shaped, green glass bottles for a nickel. Bottled Coca-Cola soon became available everywhere and to everyone, resulting in fabulous new profits for the company. But by selling the drink for the first time outside of the tightly segregated confines of the middle-class soda fountain, lower-class whites and African Americans could now get their hands on this potentially dangerous product. The consumption of Coca-Cola, and by proxy the consumption of cocaine, by these "undesirables"—black men in particular—thus contributed to the next step in the cultural transformation of cocaine, this time from a necessary yet controllable medical tool to a threatening social menace.

"THE NEGRO COCAINE FIEND"

The earliest available evidence for the use of cocaine by southern African Americans can be found in the late 1880s among laborers in and around New Orleans. Like South American Indians who chewed on coca leaves while working in the mines, black dock workers used cocaine as a stimulant to help them endure the long hours and extreme exertion of loading and unloading ships. It gradually became common practice for employers to provide cocaine for their workers as part of their daily wages. From the waterfronts of New Orleans, the drug spread to levee builders and plantation workers upriver. While generating alarm over the new threat of cocaine use "filling the insane asylums with wrecks," one medical journal detailed the role of cocaine in the lives of the agricultural working class: "The planters therefore hold out every encouragement to the negro hands to put in a big day's work. The negroes found that the drug enabled them to work longer and make more money, and so they took to it." Harkening back to the antebellum plantation era, the journal concluded, "[Cocaine] use has grown steadily. On many of the Yazoo plantations this year the negroes refused to work unless they could be assured that there was some place in the neighborhood that they could get cocaine, and one big planter is reported to keep the drug in regular stock among the plantation supplies and to issue regular rations of cocaine just as he was accustomed in the past to issue rations of whiskey."[22]

In addition to using cocaine as a stimulant at work, African Americans began using the drug recreationally at about the same time. In most urban areas across the country, cocaine and other drugs were cheap and readily available in either pharmaceutical purity or in prepackaged products like nasal decongestants or cough suppressants. Cocaine in particular became a central ingredient in the nightlife of African American and interracial urban centers and red-light districts like New Orleans's Storyville or Atlanta's Decatur. An informal though not yet illegal market in cocaine emerged in these neighborhoods, supplying anyone with a dime and the taste for a kick. As jazz musician Jelly Roll Morton recalled, "Those days . . . you could buy all the dope you wanted in the drug store. Just ask for it and you got it." Lawrence Levine, a historian of African American folk culture, discovered a rich collection of argot and song celebrating "snow" and its place in black, urban jook joints and the "sportin' life":

> Coke, I love, coke, I buy,
> I'm gonna sniff my coke till the day I die,
> Hey honey, take a whiff on me.

And yet another tune took a more tragic view of the stuff:

> Well, the cocaine habit is might' bad
> It kill ev-ybody I know it to have had,
> O my babe!
> I went to the drug-store, I went in a lope;
> Sign on the door: "There's no mo' coke."
> O my babe, O my babe.[23]

These lyrics afford a rare opportunity to witness the pleasure and pain of drug use within this black urban culture. The voices of the drug users from this era are hard to find, and historians quickly find themselves trapped by a dependence upon a white written record, intent on demonizing the black drug user, that failed to document these experiences of escapism and suffering, of pleasure and warning.

Reformers and white supremacists warned of the dangers inherent in African American sources of pleasure, especially the ominous mix of sex, intoxication, jazz, and race mixing to be found in urban districts. For white reformers, these scenes generated pornographic nightmares of drunken or "doped up" black men raping white women who had been seduced by such sinful pleasures. In short, given that cocaine was known to be a powerful stimulant—erotic or otherwise—and black men were using it in public, then both the drug and its users constituted a serious threat to the stability of the Jim Crow racial order then under construction across the South.

Medical journals reported on the new "Negro cocaine menace," and newspapers across the South ran exposés on the use of cocaine by African Americans, prostitutes, and other members of the urban sporting class. In 1899 the *Chattanooga Times* investigated the use of addictive drugs and reported that only "the lowest, most criminal and depraved portion of any city's population" consumed cocaine. Shortly thereafter, archetypal stories appeared in newspapers of black cocaine users committing crimes and raping white women. "I have given the cocaine question considerable study," wrote Georgia's Colonel J. W. Watson in a northern publication in 1903, "and I am satisfied that many of the horrible crimes committed in the southern States by the colored people can be traced directly to the cocaine habit." And in New Orleans, local newspapers attributed the violent resistance of Robert Charles—whose deadly shoot out with police in 1900 led to a bloody racial massacre—to his use of cocaine.[24]

In another sensational and often retold story, police in Asheville, North Carolina, shot an African American man believed to be high on cocaine over a dozen times before finally beating the man to death with their spent service revolvers. After recounting this story in horrific detail, Edward Huntington Williams, a medical doctor, offered his professional diagnosis: "Perhaps the most interesting feature

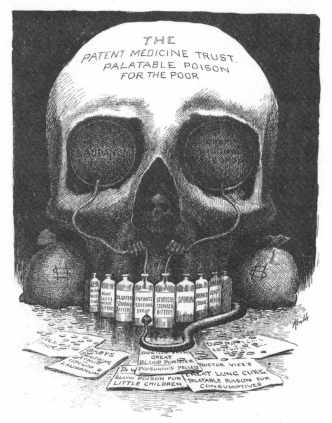

By the early twentieth century, Progressive reformers had set their sights on destroying the patent medicine industry. Cover of the muckraking magazine Collier's, *from 1905.*

of the effects of cocainism, at least from a medical standpoint, is the fact that the drug renders the user immune to shock to an astonishing degree." Williams quickly turns his physiological observations into a justification for police brutality and segregation. "In the language of the police officer, 'the cocaine nigger is sure hard to kill'—a fact that has been demonstrated so often that many of these officers in the South have increased the caliber of their guns for the express purpose of 'stopping' the cocaine fiend when he runs amuck. . . . Needless to say this immunity to shock, together with the fearlessness, hallucinations, and homicidal tendencies that cocaine engenders, makes the 'fiend' an object of special dread." This is an example of racialized thinking at its most reductive: why else would a black man lash out at the institutional agents of his oppression unless his already inferior mind and powerfully able body were under the debilitating influence of some foreign and nefarious drug?[25] Offered by the police, interpreted by a physician, and printed in the reputable *Medical Record*, this tale of an almost unstoppable, irrational monster merged the authority of scientific and police expertise into a justification for state killings and aligned the imperatives of drug regulation into a coercive pillar of white supremacy in the New South.

The initial wave of anti-black drug panic had immediate results, especially at the Coca-Cola Company. "Use of the drug among negroes is growing to an alarming extent," read a 1901 *Atlanta Constitution* article. "It is stated that quite a number of the soft drinks dispensed at soda fountains contain cocaine, and that these drinks serve to unconsciously cultivate the habit." Clearly, Candler could not have his product tainted by the mythologized stigma of race riot and black rapists. Beginning in 1901, he quietly charged his company chemists with removing the coca extract from Coca-Cola, compensating by fortifying the drink with sugar and huge doses of the increasingly popular stimulant caffeine. Candler also began to deny, often under oath, that Coca-Cola had ever contained cocaine, thus establishing official company mythology that remains entrenched to this day. Although Coca-Cola did, for a time, lose customers to its many "cocanized" competitors, Candler had the shrewd business sense to change with the prevailing winds and thereby ensure that the Coca-Cola company would be one of the few patent-medicine manufacturers to survive the Progressive era. By the time race riots rocked Atlanta in 1906 and white supremacists again blamed the riots on pinches of cocaine sold in whiskey shots, Coca-Cola had escaped the taint of association and blame.[26]

At the same time that Candler quietly changed his secret formula, local lawmakers and law enforcement across the South moved to outlaw the "Negro cocaine menace." Most southern states—starting with Georgia, Tennessee, and Florida—enacted total bans on cocaine in the first three years of the twentieth century, twelve years before the federal government began to even regulate the drug. The central role played by race in southern drug reform must be underscored by the fact that cocaine faced a complete ban, and cocaine users—universally assumed to be black—confronted prison time nearly a decade before any southern state took similar action against opium, morphine, or heroin, the drugs of choice for most white addicts in the South.

While the law sharply emphasized the public indulgences of black cocaine users, it did nothing to expose the drug use of whites, the Mrs. Henry Layfayette Duboses of the South, enabling them to legally support their morphine and heroin addictions behind a stifling curtain of middle-class civility and feminine domesticity. In a sense, the South's first war on drugs was simply a criminal-medical adaptation of the logic of Jim Crow itself: the uncontrollability of black sexuality required the repressive politics of white men to protect—and thereby contain—the pristine inviolability of white southern womanhood. Forged within the sexual politics of Jim Crow, racial repression and drug prohibition formed two sides of the same coin, and the double standard of acceptable and unacceptable drug use was minted.

ENTER THE PROGRESSIVES

In the development of U.S. drug-control laws, the South, guided by its Jim Crow political logic, proved itself far in advance of the rest of the nation when it came to pressing forward with drug prohibition, but the other states proved quick to catch on. Federal laws reforming the use of drugs in the United States are commonly viewed as one of the untrammeled successes of the Progressive era, especially the contributions of the anti-patent-medicine muckraker Samuel Hopkins Adams and the passage of the 1906 Pure Food and Drug Act. But this period of reason and reform was also fraught with racial conflicts and redefinitions: northern na-tivists battled against the flood of immigrant Catholics and Jews, western whites attacked the Chinese with legal bans and racist pogroms, the South enshrined Jim Crow disenfranchisement and segregation in their state constitutions, and the na-tion as a whole took up its own piece of the white man's burden in its imperialist expansion into the Caribbean and the Philippines. In this racially and religiously charged climate, the war on drugs became a unifying element in a crusade for racial, moral, and national purity. In the eyes of powerful reformers, foreign drugs were—like aspiring immigrants and African Americans—being mixed with and polluting the body politic, contributing to what Teddy Roosevelt warned was the "race suicide" of white Americans. This racialized, sexualized, and moral-inter-ventionist approach to drug control created the belief that narcotics and cocaine represented a single threat to which a unified, inflexible, and uncompromising ban was the only proper solution. There was to be no such thing as an acceptable level of public drug use in U.S. society. In the process, Americans demonized drug addicts for the first time, denouncing "dope fiends" who must be coercively controlled as a criminal population. Moral hardliners beat back every effort, including the experimental maintenance clinics, to treat drug addiction as a medical or health-related problem. In the end, progress in this newly declared war on drugs came to be measured by the list of substances banned, the quantity of local, state, and federal laws passed, and the number of newly criminalized people incarcerated under its provisions.

By 1913 reformers felt the time was ripe to push for uniform federal antidrug laws. Southern lawmakers dusted off their now ten-year-old horror stories of black rape and riot in a new campaign to convince a national audience of the social menace represented by cocaine. The September 29, 1913, headline in the virulently antidrug Hearst chain of newspapers read,

10 KILLED, 35 HURT IN A RACE RIOT BORN OF A COCAINE DRUNK
Drug Crazed Negroes Fire at Everyone in Sight in Mississippi Town
THREE WHITE MEN AMONG THE DEAD
One of the Brothers Who Started Shooting Lynched, Other Dies in Battle
Guardsmen Restore Order

The medical press also repeated their long-held professional recommendations for regulating cocaine by attesting to the inferiority of African Americans and

Hamilton Wright (here), America's first "Drug Czar," knew that he needed the white South's support for his federal antidrug legislation. Recognizing that racial fears could outweigh states' rights skepticism, he asserted that "cocaine is often the direct incentive to the crime of rape by the negroes of the South" — and therefore had to be controlled. Photograph courtesy of the Collections of the Library of Congress.

the special danger they posed when possessed by cocaine. Edward Huntington Williams wrote in the *New York Times* that doctors had authoritatively determined the following biological science:

> Once the negro has reached the stage of being a "dope taker"—and a very few experimental sniffs of the drug make him an habitué—he is a constant menace to his community until he is eliminated. For his whole nature is changed for the worse by the habit. Sexual desires are increased and perverted, peaceful negroes become quarrelsome, and timid negroes develop a degree of "Dutch courage" that is sometimes almost incredible. A large proportion of the wholesale killings in the South during recent years have been the direct result of cocaine. Moreover, the negro who has once formed the habit, seems absolutely beyond redemption. Imprisonment "cures" him temporarily; but when released he returns to the drug almost inevitably.[27]

In this fashion, the North, previously concerned only with restricting opium-smoking and heroin, quickly learned from southern Progressives that cocaine was perhaps a greater social menace than anything they had experienced.

The myth of the black cocaine fiend effectively united southern white supremacists and northern Progressives behind a common plan. Advocating for federal drug control, the *New York Times* argued that only national laws could protect the South from its cocaine problem: "Nearly all the Southern States have taken drastic measures to prevent the sale of cocaine, but until the Federal Government takes a hand by prohibiting the movement of drugs in inter-state commerce, a great deal will be smuggled across state lines and used." This argument is curious in its implication that the North has a responsibility to help its southern neighbors protect their system of segregation by working to keep cocaine out of the hands of African Americans. Senator Ben Tillman of South Carolina, one of southern politics most outspoken advocates of Jim Crow and states' rights, agreed with this logic and campaigned on behalf of federal drug laws because, in his words, drugs "are causing so much trouble among the negroes." Federal drug control laws, therefore, did not represent an intervention in the southern system of Jim Crow but a powerful tool to help bolster and protect it.[28]

During the legislative session of 1914, Hamilton Wright—a physician, international drug control negotiator for the U.S. State Department, and the nation's first "Drug Czar"—composed a federal antidrug law that would ban the distribution of heroin, morphine, and cocaine without a doctor's prescription. Wright delegated the work of shepherding the bill through Congress to the capable Francis Burton Harrison, a wealthy Tammany Democrat; however, Wright knew that southern support for the bill was essential, especially in a year in which Democrats had captured the White House and both houses of Congress. It was widely believed that such a federal intervention into southern law enforcement would be seen as an affront to the traditional states' rights views of southern Democrats, but Wright also knew that if he could demonstrate that southern leadership was essential to the fashioning of the bill's provisions and that the bill was explicitly deploying the racial proscriptions of Jim Crow on a national level, then southern Democrats would fall in line behind their party, their president, and the racial politics that kept them all in power. Thus Wright, a highly educated physican, diplomat, and enthusiastic bearer of the white man's burden in the Philippines and China, could testify before Congress with compelling conviction that "it has been authoritatively stated that cocaine is often the direct incentive to the crime of rape by the negroes of the South."[29] After some legislative wrangling and final approval by the American Medical Association and the American Pharmaceutical Association, Congress passed the Harrison Anti-Narcotics Act of 1914.

In the history of Progressivism, the South is usually seen as a poor and backwards region in need of scientific and managerial uplift from its more sophisticated neighbors in the North. But as the story of U.S. drug prohibition demonstrates, the South was in fact a major contributor to the formation of a national reform agenda. This is especially significant because the turn of the century represents the moment of the South's greatest confidence in its system of racial apartheid—a system that whites believed functioned so well, it could be recommended with pride and successfully exported for the rest of the nation to adopt when dealing with its own problems of race and social control. Thus, when it came time for the United States to declare its first war on drugs during the Progressive era, the South's racial politics fused with broad national anxieties about race and immigration to shape dramatically not only U.S. public policy but also the nation's moral judgments about drugs as well. Today, when over three quarters of the men and women in federal prisons on felony drug charges are people of color, far exceeding their percentage of either the overall population or the drug-using segment, this legacy remains as potent as ever.[30] Indeed, the poisoned fruit of our ongoing war on drugs has deep roots in American history, and it remains one of the most persistent and pernicious legacies of Jim Crow.

NOTES

1. "Drugs Sap Nation's Vigor," *New York Times*, 19 February 1911, 12.

2. On race and the political history of whiteness see Mathew Frye Jacobson, *Whiteness of a Different Color: European Immigrants and the Alchemy of Race* (Harvard University Press, 1998), 39–90.

3. F. F. Kane, *Opium Smoking in America and China* (1887; rprt. Arno Press Reprints, 1974); Norman H. Clark, *Deliver Us from Evil: An Interpretation of American Prohibition* (Norton, 1976); Charles H. Whitebread and Richard J. Bonnie, *The Marijuana Conviction: A History of Marijuana Prohibition in the United States* (Lindesmith Center, 1999); Harry J. Anslinger, "Marijuana, Assassin of Youth," *The American Magazine* (July 1937): 18–19, 150–53.

4. "Negro Cocaine Fiends," *Medical News* 81 (November 1902): 895.

5. Harper Lee, *To Kill a Mockingbird* (J.B. Lippencott Co., 1960), 99–112.

6. David T. Courtwright, "The Hidden Epidemic: Opiate Addiction and Cocaine Use in the South, 1860–1920," *The Journal of Southern History* 49.1 (February 1983): 57–72.

7. David F. Musto, *The American Disease, Origins of Narcotics Control*, 3RD ed. (Oxford University Press, 1999), 91–182; Lawrence Kolb and A. G. Du Metz, "The Prevalence and Trend of Drug Addiction in the United States and the Factors Influencing It," *Public Health Reports* 29.21 (May 1924): 1179–1204; Charles Terry, "Drug Addictions, a Public Health Problem," *American Journal of Public Health* 4 (January 1914): 28–37; Lucius P. Brown, "Enforcement of the Tennessee Anti-Narcotics Law," *American Journal of Public Health* 5 (1915): 323–33.

8. William L. White, *Slaying the Dragon: The History of Addiction Treatment and Recovery in America* (Chestnutt Health, 1998).

9. "Quackery and the Quacked," *National Quarterly Review* (1861), quoted in Musto, *American Disease*, 301; on the history of American quackery, see James Harvey Young, *American Health Quackery: Collected Essays by James Harvey Young* (Princeton University Press, 1992).

10. "Many Doctors Drug Users," *New York Times*, 6 March 1911; Lyman F. Kebler, "The Dope Evil: From a Statistician's Point of View" (1911), in *American Perceptions of Drug Addiction: Five Studies 1872–1912*, ed. Gerald N. Grob (Arno Press Reprints, 1981).

11. Stephen Kandall, *Substance and Shadow: Women and Addiction in the United States* (Harvard University Press, 1996); Mara L. Keire, "Dope Fiends and Degenerates: The Gendering of Drug Addiction in the Early Twentieth Century," *Journal of Social History* 31.4 (Summer 1998): 809–22; Eugene O'Neill, *Long Day's Journey into Night* (Yale University Press, 1956), 74.

12. Todd L. Savitt and James Harvey Young, eds., *Disease and Distinctiveness in the American South* (University of Tennessee Press, 1988); David T. Courtwright, "Opiate Addiction as a Consequence of the Civil War," *Civil War History* 24 (Fall 1978): 101–11; William A. Owens, *This Stubborn Soil: A Frontier Childhood* (Charles Scribner, 1966), 6–8.

13. L. C. Allen, "Negro Health Problems," *American Journal of Public Health* 5 (March 1915); Susan Lynn Smith, *Sick and Tired of Being Sick and Tired: Black Women's Health Activism in America, 1890–1950* (University of Pennsylvania Press, 1995); Tera W. Hunter, *To 'Joy My Freedom': Southern Black Women's Lives and Labors after the Civil War* (Harvard University Press, 1997), especially chapter 9; and Katherine Bankole, *Slavery and Medicine: Enslavement and Medical Practices in Antebellum Louisiana* (Garland Press, 1998).

14. James Harvey Young, *The Toadstool Millionaires: A Social History of Patent Medicines in America before Federal Regulation* (Princeton University Press, 1961) On patent-medicine advertising, see A. Walker Bingham, *The Snake Oil Syndrome: Patent Medicine Advertising* (Christopher Publishing House, 1994); and Jackson Lears, *Fables of Abundance: A Cultural History of Advertising in America* (Basic Books, 1994), 137–54.

15. James Harvey Young, "Three Atlanta Pharmacists," *Pharmacy in History* 31.1 (1989): 16–22.

16. Monroe Martin King, "Dr. John S. Pemberton: Originator of Coca-Cola," *Pharmacy in History* 29.2 (1987): 85–89.

17. Quoted in Mark Pendergrast, *For God, For Country and Coca-Cola: The Unauthorized History of the Great American Soft Drink and the Company That Makes It* (Charles Scribner, 1993), 26–27.

18. On the rise of southern consumer culture see Grace Elizabeth Hale, *Making Whiteness: The Culture of Segregation in the South, 1890–1940* (Vintage Books, 1998), 122–97.

19. "What's In Coca Cola? A Popular Drink Which is Said to Foster the Cocaine Habit," *Atlanta Constitution*, 21 June 1891.

20. Joseph F. Spillane, *Cocaine: From Medical Marvel to Modern Menace in the United States, 1884–1920* (Johns Hopkins University Press, 2000), 90–122.

21. Pendergrast, *For God, For Country and Coca-Cola*, 58.

22. "Negro Cocaine Fiends," *Medical News* 81 (8 November 1902): 895; Spillane, *Cocaine,* 91–93.

23. Quoted in Lawrence Levine, *Black Culture and Black Consciousness: Afro-American Folk Thought From Slavery to Freedom* (Oxford University Press 1977), 283.

24. "This Drug-Endangered Nation," *Literary Digest,* 28 March 1914, 687; "Cocaine Fiends," *Chattanooga Times,* 11 October 1899; Jeffrey Clayton Foster, "The Rocky Road to a 'Drug Free Tennessee': A History of the Early Regulation of Cocaine and the Opiates, 1897–1913," *Journal of Social History* (Spring 1996): 547–46; "Cocaine Sniffers," New York *Daily Tribune,* 21 June 1903; William Ivy Hair, *Carnival of Fury: Robert Charles and the New Orleans Race Riot of 1900* (Louisiana State University, 1976), 76–78.

25. Edward Huntington Williams, "The Drug Habit Menace in the South," *Medical Record,* 7 February 1914, 247–49; on the sexual politics of Jim Crow see Glenda E. Gilmore, *Gender and Jim Crow: Women and the Politics of White Supremacy in North Carolina 1896–1920* (University of North Carolina Press, 1996), 31–118.

26. "Cocaine Is Sold Illegally," *Atlanta Constitution,* 20 November 1901; on the Atlanta race riot of 1906, see Joel Williamson, *A Rage for Order: Black/White Relations in the American South Since Emancipation* (Oxford University Press, 1986), 141–51.

27. *New York Herald,* 29 September 1913, 1; Edward Huntington Williams, "Negro Cocaine 'Fiends' New Southern Menace," *New York Times,* 8 February 1914.

28. "Nations Uniting to Stamp Out the Use of Opium and Many Other Drugs," *New York Times,* 25 July 1909; Ben Tillman quoted in Williams, *Rage for Order,* 142.

29. Quoted in Musto, *The American Disease,* 43–44.

30. Statistical data on the current drug war and incarceration rates in the United States are published by The Sentencing Project, at http://www.sentencingproject.org, accessed on 13 April 2006.

Lacy Charm in Old Mobile
The Historic Cast Iron of Alabama's First City

by John Sledge
Photography by Sheila Hagler

The McCoy House (1873) verandah at 253 State Street features mixed elements. The columns and heavy Gothic brackets are from one foundry, while the railing with its anthemions is from another. The brackets' manufacturer recommended a different railing, but for some reason the owner preferred this one. All photographs by Sheila Hagler.

Visitors frequently refer to Mobile's historic ironwork as wrought iron, but the majority of it is cast iron. Cast iron, cheap and easy to produce in an infinite variety of shapes and designs, captured the imagination of nineteenth-century tastemakers seeking dramatic effect. Virtually every American city accessible by water had some ornamental cast iron, but it was nowhere more exuberantly employed than in the Deep South, particularly the Gulf ports, where wooden structures too rapidly succumbed to the semitropical climate.

Whether locally designed and manufactured or imported from big East Coast foundries, Mobile's nineteenth-century ornamental ironwork nicely exhibits the era's diverse aesthetic tastes. A Greek Revival gate, a Gothic-accented cemetery fence, a town house verandah with arabesque patterns, a plashing fountain distinguished by satyr's faces — Mobilians' enthusiasm for the practical advantages and decorative delights of these things flourished until the turn of the twentieth century.

Today, after decades of indifference and neglect, Mobilians once again appreciate the historic ironwork in their midst. Restored balconies are more popular than ever with residents, office workers, diners, and Mardi Gras revelers eager to take in the passing scene; fluted lamps illumine downtown streets; and venerable fences, gates, and statuary gleam with fresh coats of paint. Though a heartbreaking amount of Mobile's ornamental ironwork has been lost or stolen over the years, what remains continues to fascinate visitors and residents alike.

Ed. note: John Sledge and Sheila Hagler share this portrait of historic cast iron décor in Mobile, Alabama, from their new book, An Ornament to the City: Old Mobile Ironwork *(University of Georgia Press, 2006). For more information visit www.ugapress.org.*

Sambo (left), manufactured by the Philadelphia foundry of Wood and Perot as a hitching post, is a rare piece which has had a troubled history in Alabama's Port City. At present it rests peacefully outside the National African American Archives, 564 Martin Luther King, Jr. Avenue. The gates and fence (below) at Barton Academy (1836), 504 Government Street, are an eloquent manifestation of neoclassicism in iron. This is among Mobile's earliest surviving ironwork.

The Bienville Square fountain (1890) was dedicated to Dr. George A. Ketchum, president of the Bienville Water Works and an advocate of a pure water supply. Existing records do not indicate the fountain's origin, but the bottom basin exactly matches others fabricated by the J. L. Mott Ironworks, New York. Cast iron setters such as this one (left) at the Stephen Twelves plot (1860) in Magnolia Cemetery were especially popular in nineteenth-century cemeteries, where they represented loyalty and individuals' love of their pets.

The Richards House
(1860), an Italianate
mansion at 256 North
Joachim Street, represents
cast iron's apogee in
Mobile. The hearts and
floral flourishes of the
porch railing (above)
demonstrate the degree of
craftsmanship achieved
by mid-nineteenth-century
founders. The house
also is dramatically
demarcated from the
sidewalk by one of the
best-preserved cast iron
residential fences (left)
in the city. Richards was
a wealthy steamboat
captain from Maine.

*The Lyon House
(1860) verandah mixes
disparate patterns in
riotous excess (above).
Lacy brackets, drop
friezes, and pendants
dazzle the eye. The gate
below bars entrance to
an unknown plot in
Magnolia Cemetery.
The lovely floral pattern
was popular during
the 1850s.*

This modern downtown hotel (left),
constructed during the 1960s, employs under-
scaled reproduction ironwork in an attempt to
capitalize on Mobile's distinctive sense of place.
The gallery at the Butt-Frazier House (below)
used ironwork cast by a local foundry in 1897
and represents one of the latest residential
iron galleries in the city.

The Richards House (1860) has a spectacular verandah (left), which includes allegorical figures of the four seasons, arabesques, hearts, and intricately intertwined tendrils. The fence (below, in detail) at the Stephen Twelves plot (1860) in Magnolia Cemetery is another example of how Victorian Mobilians fell in love with cast iron's decorative possibilities.

An example of the Port City's most beautiful ornamental ironwork, the Slatter Mausoleum (1860) and its surrounding Gothic Revival fence (left) in Magnolia Cemetery were ordered by a cotton factor. The gates (1860) at the Cathedral of the Immaculate Conception (below) at 4 S. Claiborne Street communicate ecclesiastical function through the crosses atop the posts, the trefoils along the bottom border, and the wreathed "AM" motifs at the center of each gate, which signify Ave Maria.

Film

Twenty-First-Century Slavery
Or, How to Extend the Confederacy
for Two Centuries Beyond Its
Planned Demise

C.S.A.: The Confederate States of America
directed by Kevin Willmott

REVIEWED BY TRUDIER HARRIS

In a series of vignettes, with the thread of a single white family's involvement in slavery holding Willmott's film together, C.S.A. moves through scenes of slavery, war, Reconstruction, imperialist expansion, domestic crises, imagined post-slavery slavery, and contemporary politics. Commercials offer viewers ways of keeping their slaves docile (including behavior-altering pills in more contemporary times), aids to their cleaning work (the Gold Dust Twins), pleasure whose logos are identified with blacks ("Niggerhead Tobacco"), toothpaste commercials ("Sambo Bright"), and advice on tracking blacks suffering from the dreaded runaway disease. Poster courtesy of IFC Films and C.S.A.

C.S.A.: The Confederate States of America, conceived and filmed by Kevin Willmott and presented by Spike Lee, is a mockumentary—that is, a film designed to spoof various historical television documentaries, especially work in the vein of that of Ken Burns. An extended contemplation of what it would have meant to the western hemisphere if the American South had won the Civil War, *C.S.A.* was ostensibly made by a British company and is replete with the requisite commercials of a television production. These are sometimes as innocuous as the one featuring a father who protects his family with Confederate Insurance and as insidious as the one advertising a bracelet designed to let modern day paddyrollers know the exact location of any "buck" who dares to run away.

Following other established patterns, the film includes talking heads—a black woman and a white man—who shed light on the actions being narrated and who put the history in perspective (chosen, the filmmaker asserted in a Birmingham premier, to mirror historians Barbara Fields and Shelby Foote in one of Burns's films). The black female scholar is Canadian, while the white male commentator, with his consistent lamenting of and apologies for the good ole days, appears to be an American of the traditional stripe. The Canadian connection is significant, for Canada is represented as the progressive, integrated society that its neighbor to the South has woefully failed to become. In Canada, blacks, fully integrated into the culture, have achieved grand things in society and the professions, while their counterparts to the South are still cooking, cleaning, and taking care of children. This selection of Canada evokes an historical pattern for African Americans, one in which, when northern escape attempts were stymied by the Fugitive Slave Law of 1850, they proceeded into Canadian territories and established communities there. Such communities are still in existence in places such as Nova Scotia.

In a series of vignettes, with the thread of a single white family's involvement in slavery holding the film together, *C.S.A.* moves through scenes of slavery, war, Reconstruction, imperialist expansion, domestic crises, imagined post-slavery slavery, and contemporary politics. Commercials offer viewers ways of keeping their slaves docile (including behavior-altering pills in more contemporary times), aids to their cleaning work (the Gold Dust Twins), pleasure whose logos are identified with blacks ("Niggerhead Tobacco"), toothpaste commercials ("Sambo Bright"), advice on tracking blacks suffering from the dreaded runaway disease ("draptomania"), employment opportunities in "Slavery Illnesses," a television auction in the vein of the Shopping Channel (in which an entire family can be purchased together or separately), and a host of other equally offensive—though at times humorous—plays on the misery of enslaved persons.

C.S.A. shamelessly and humorously rewrites history to achieve its objective. Abraham Lincoln, for example, is portrayed as defeated and, in an attempt to escape his potential Confederate captors, calls upon Harriet Tubman, the consummate liberator, to get him to free territory. She agrees to help him by asserting, "Mr. Lincoln, we're both niggers now." Lincoln dons blackface, and the two begin their escape. However, in a scene reminiscent of D. W. Griffith's *The Birth of a Nation*, in which captions on the screen and jerky camera movement carry the action, Lincoln and Tubman are "smelled" out by a trusty Confederate who wipes the makeup off Lincoln. Caught in such an ignominious position, Lincoln is exiled to Canada, where, shortly before his death in 1905, he gives an interview expressing regret that he could not free blacks in traditional America.

In another rewriting of history, abolitionists who learn that the South has won the war and who realize that they can no longer work successfully toward the liberation of blacks in America migrate to Canada. They include Walt Whitman, William Lloyd Garrison, Frederick Douglass, Susan B. Anthony, and a host of others. In Canada, Anthony gets the vote for women at least a decade before that objective was achieved historically in America.

In its fictitious narrative, the film posits that, once the South won the Civil War, it proceeded to conquer Mexico, Latin America, and South America, therefore actualizing a situation in which "America" indeed referred to the majority of the territory in this hemisphere. While Mexicans are not enslaved, they are forced to endure what blacks in the South experienced in the early twentieth century as

At one point C.S.A. *is even reminiscent of D. W. Griffith's* The Birth of a Nation, *in which captions on the screen and jerky camera movement carry the action. Scene from* The Birth of a Nation, *courtesy of the Museum of Modern Art Film Stills Archive.*

signs go up in public facilities for "Blancos" and others. In one especially humorous scene, a Spanish-speaking talking head laments the conquest in gastronomic terms, as he recounts being forced to eat sandwiches and some horror called "chitterlings."

On the traditionally American domestic front, one family dominates the political arena. One ancestor was in the Civil War, another was instrumental in a plot to remove all Jews from the Confederate States, and still another collaborated with Hitler. In the early twenty-first century, Fauntroy the Fifth is a candidate for President of the United States before forces arrayed against him bring charges that he has colored ancestry. Threatened with being called before the Bureau of Racial Identity, which has the responsibility of determining purity in race, Fauntroy the Fifth commits suicide. Ironically, the DNA that he has refused to give to clear his name while alive reveals after his death that he was indeed "pure white."

With this constant bombardment of images, storylines, plots, subplots, and talking heads, viewers are perhaps at a loss occasionally as to what to make of all this. The South won the Civil War, conquered most of the western world, and still has slavery in the twenty-first century. All of that might be appalling—or not, depending on the viewer—but one is still left to ponder Willmott's ultimate purpose. Certainly the spoofing is well done, and certainly there is humor in what he offers viewers. Still, many questions arise. Does Willmott simply want to generate conversation? Is the film just about the various "What if . . . ?" possibilities that could have occurred in American history? Is the film designed to shame some viewers and uplift others? Is this a test of the limits of filmmaking and potential censorship? Is it the starting point for discussion of the *real* twenty-first century slavery, that is, the continual exploitation of people of color who are born in America or enter its borders? Are blacks to be proud of the film? Or is it just an expansive, self-indulgent joke that goes on too long? I came away from the film with lots of images floating in my head but with the distinct impression that I stopped laughing *long* before the film ended. For me, therefore, the film's epigraph ultimately failed—that is, that humor must be used to tell people the truth, or otherwise they will kill you.

Two larger issues also arise—those of black voice and black bodies. While the black woman talking head offers quite a bit of commentary, most of the blacks shown in the film are without voice. (With a few notable exceptions: the black servant who asserts that Fauntroy the Fifth has black blood in his family and a vignette featuring an Aunt Thomasina who tells on a black man planning to run away. The latter is in one of the commercials.) As they are shepherded to various locations, black bodies may grimace, run, or writhe in pain, but they are mostly silent. They stand on auction blocks, cook, clean, hang out clothes, and provide subject matter for the various "slavery illnesses," but again they are mostly silent.

In another example of the film's rewriting of history, abolitionists who learn that the South has won the war and who realize that they can no longer work successfully toward the liberation of blacks in America migrate to Canada. They include Walt Whitman, William Lloyd Garrison, Susan B. Anthony, Frederick Douglass (here), and a host of others. Frontispiece photograph from Life and Times of Frederick Douglass, *published by De Wolfe & Fiske in Boston.*

Does this mean, then, that most blacks were/are acquiescent in their own enslavement? Does this mean that resistance to slavery was minimal? Does it mean that enslaved blacks simply waited for others to speak for them? The film inadvertently runs the risk of *seeming to posit* that blacks during slavery were, with a few exceptions, rather satisfied with their conditions. Everybody has a narrative about them, but they themselves do not tell their own story.

Yet, black bodies are gloriously present, so much so that one cannot miss the sexual overtones attached to them. For example, a stripped-to-the-waist black male appears in the "draptomania" commercial. Although he has nodes connected to his body in a medical experiment, it is nonetheless apparent that he is a "prime buck," who seems to have no objection to showing the whites studying him how fast he can run on a treadmill. Similarly, a stripped-to-the-waist black male is the father of the family featured in the Shopping Channel-like commercial sequence, which is hosted by two white females. Their "oohs" and "aahs" of appreciation for this "piece" of black male flesh certainly deserve remarking. They evoke a host of psychosexual associations between black males and white females that are even more highlighted by the film's context.

Slavery as a phenomenon in any society is undoubtedly worthy of commentary, as is the hypocrisy affiliated with it. After all, the South is able to persuade northerners to buy into continued slavery after Reconstruction because they convince them of the personal advantages that will accrue to them once they embrace slavery. Nonetheless, approaching such an emotional issue in the at times light-hearted manner that Willmott does invites lingering and unsettling responses to his endeavor. Although he includes a trailer showing how the various products depicted in the "commercials" in the film were once actually part of American culture (à la the documentary *Ethnic Notions*), there is still at times a sense of moving backward instead of going forward. But perhaps even that, as William Faulkner and Toni Morrison argue, is the only path by which societies can truly move into the future. Yet, *C.S.A.* leaves me with the aggravating sense of popcorn in my teeth. I tongue it and tongue it in an effort to dislodge it, but the persistent little bugger just keeps hanging around. Only the full attention of focusing on the film directly—with repeated and earnest conversations—will dislodge the hold it has on me and the viewers with whom I shared responses. Those conversations won't transcend American history, but they might at least move us to a healthier place in contemplating it.

I'm Talking about Shaft

BY MICHAEL PARKER

"In some ways 'Shaft' is a ridiculously over-the-top song. Those twittering flutes, the heavy drapery of strings, foretold the arrival of dreaded disco and connected the song to first cousins like 'You Don't Have to Be a Star, Baby (To Be in My Show)' rather than the more desirable kinfolk of the mid-sixties Stax-Volt catalog, to which Isaac Hayes lent his brilliant songwriting and production skills. But though there is a direct line from 'Shaft' to the schmaltziest ballads of the Bee Gees, something erupts in my thighs when I hear the high-hat cymbal tick and that introductory wah-wah scratch guitar." Isaac Hayes, courtesy of http://www.isaachayes.com/.

Butterball Thompson's the one forgot to pivot right that fateful night, wedging our lameass squad right up into the foursome of skinny flutists stopped in front of us on the halftime-show football field. Stick girls, their band uniforms turning their slat-thin bodies into boneless black and gold garment bags, drooping from shoulder to spat without a clue of womanly curve. Our uniforms weren't exactly designed to highlight anatomical assets. My own was just as slack, but my squad mates — Butterball on Tuba, Winifred Hammerman on the trombone, and Cedrick Raynor playing, like me, the baritone horn — were all straining in their duds. Cedrick wore where-the-flood pants that crept up his shin with each goose step. Winnie Hammer, when he extended the arm of his trombone to distant position, flashed a good six inches of white dress shirt sleeve. Butterball, got dog, man — he was button-popping, stuffed up in that uniform, his girth calling into question whether he ought to suffer such bodily restraint and be expected to blow big and solemn low-down notes on the tuba. Butter, like most big boys, had this slow, easy, solid thing going — he moved up underwater to a soundtrack by the Chi-Lites — and seeing him bound and trussed, every damn thing, even the spats squeezing his feet, hampering his considerable chops on the tuba, made you want to get all politically active, plead cruel and inhumane, sign some petition demanding: Free Big Butter!

Ours was the worst squad in the Clinton, North Carolina, high school marching band. We were screw-ups who could not cut it in other squads, so the director, nicknamed Belly, after his considerable paunch, put us together, thus quadrupling our inefficiency and igniting all sorts of mid-field "Your Mama" trash talk. Our band was one of the best in the state, despite the fact that our musical repertoire was resolutely lame: the inexplicably titled Chicago hit "25 or 6 to 4," "Theme from 'A Man Called Horse'," "Spinning Wheel." I was the lone white member of my squad and subject therefore to torrents of white-people jokes and cracks about the band Chicago and the exact meaning of a lame title like "25 or 6 to 4," which I relished. Butterball: What kind of clock do he got? Cedrick: Fool need to learn how to tell some time. Winnie: His ass definitely gone be late.

The local schools had only been integrated for three or four years, and though I found my minority status in the screw-up squad slightly uncomfortable at times, I was also thrilled by it. I'd had black friends in grade school, but the screw-up squad was my first full immersion in black culture, which I found far less provincial than my own. The great migration of rural southern blacks to the urban north was still going on in the early seventies, and I found fascinating the mysterious geographical patterns established by the blacks in my town, who tended to end up in the industrial towns of the Hudson River Valley — Newburgh and Kingston and Troy — while blacks from towns just a few miles away migrated to Baltimore or Philly. (Everyone, it seemed, had people in Brooklyn, a fact verified by the obituaries in the local newspaper.) While all of us white boys stayed put in

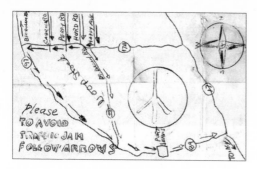

the summer, cropping tobacco for cigarette money, my black friends went north or their city cousins came south, and they brought back fashion, slang, music. I envied them their up-to-dateness, though it also put me off. Everything seemed ephemeral, if not downright disposable. By the time I learned the slang, it was no longer in circulation. White culture moved glacially—the sixties arrived one day in winter 1973, ushered in by a crusty van with Arizona tags piloted by an older freak named Jimmy Green and his younger brother, Chris. We were still listening daily to "Stairway to Heaven" two years after it came out. From Butter and crew I learned that a song as classic and timeless as, say, the O'Jays' "Love Train" had only a window of a few weeks, after which it was dismissed as "old."

Marching with Butter and Cedrick and Winnie, marveling at their ability to remain au courant in a town of scarcely seven thousand people, I felt even more keenly my lack of fulfillment. Something huge needed to happen. I needly badly to be a part of this something huge. These were the last purely hopeful months before my restlessness turned dark and my rebellion broke out in a typically early seventies self-destructive stripe. I was still innocent enough that football games on Friday nights crisply autumnal enough to render sufferable the summer-weight wool of the uniform brought out in me a fierce, if wistful, desire. I loved not the game, which I only occasionally paid attention to, or the embarrassingly dated songs we played, but the loud public spectacle of the event, which for rival teams drew huge crowds. A few years earlier I had spent a summer listening to all six sides of Woodstock and pretending I was there, among the freaks, instead of camped out on the floor of the living room, upside the air-conditioning vent, memorizing the between-songs patter of Chip Monck, who warned festival goers of bad acid circulating. Ever since, I had been into crowds.

Woodstock was not an option. The Dark Horse stadium on a chilly October night would have to do, but it was not doing it for me. I longed for a bigger stadium, brighter lights, louder drum and bass echo bouncing off the field house. My life felt as constricting as Big Butter's uniform. Yet I seemed to adhere to a philosophy that, thirty years later, seems to have changed little. Rather than go out and seek adventure, I tread water, watch, wait. I don't know if this is a failing or a kind of cunning. I only know that even the most seemingly static life is full of opportunities, small and random though they may seem when you sit back and wait for them, and that when people talk about going out there and making things happen, I am reminded of the brash, late-night swagger of infomercials, of televised workout shows led by the way buff but hopelessly vacant. But having waited so long for something to drift by, I usually find it hard not to fling myself at the jetsam. Which is what happened when Belly, one afternoon in the overheated band room, passed out the sheet music from the movie *Shaft* and announced we would be "working it up" for our halftime Homecoming routine.

I'll never know what possessed a man whose idea of the counterculture was Neil Diamond to choose not only a song still played on the radio but one that stopped just a syllable shy of uttering the word "motherfucker." I only know that I needed something to send me, and that "Theme from *Shaft*" would surely do. In some ways "*Shaft*" is a ridiculously over-the-top song. Those twittering flutes, the heavy drapery of strings, foretold the arrival of dreaded disco and connected the song to first cousins like "You Don't Have to Be a Star, Baby (To Be in My Show)" rather than the more desirable kinfolk of the mid-sixties Stax-Volt catalog, to which Isaac Hayes lent his brilliant songwriting and production skills. But though there is a direct line from "*Shaft*" to the schmaltziest ballads of the Bee Gees, something erupts in my thighs when I hear the high-hat cymbal tick and that introductory wah-wah scratch guitar. Call it slow-twitch muscle memory stirred from a thirty-year slumber. Cheesiness notwithstanding, "*Shaft*" is high on up there on the list of songs impossible to sit still through.

We worked on it for a few weeks in fourth-period band. Belly added some after-school sessions as the date drew closer, and a couple of times I even took my horn home to practice. For weeks, my lips tasted of mouthpiece: metal, spit, the musty innards of a brass instrument. The arrangement itself took some getting used to. Take away that heavily reverbed chugging guitar, add clarinet and tuba and by god hand-held bells, and you're left with, well, "*Shaft*" as interpreted by a high school marching band. But underneath all the compromises lurked that beat, which we—or at least I—were counting on propelling us to Dark Horse marching band history. Our previous halftime shows had featured such anthems as "Sweet Georgia Brown" and, at their hippest, "The Age of Aquarius." The latter seemed to highlight the ridiculously segregated state of our school, our town, the coastal plain, the state, the South, the whole damn country. The first part, "The Age of Aquarius," drew stiff nods from the whites in the audience, but when, midway through, the song slid into the funkier, looser "Let the Sunshine In," it was as if the power had been switched back on; the grandstand, where all the blacks sat, ignited in a loose sway, and the handclapping nearly drowned us out.

Now we were about to premiere, for an audience suspecting more anemic halftime show standards, the hottest jam of the Black Moses, Mr. Hot Buttered Soul himself. I envisioned the entire crowd, especially the grandstand, erupting in riotous ass-shake when we laid down that inimitable, high-hat cymbal-ticking introduction.

When, finally, Belly felt we had the song down enough to put it together with our routine, he allowed us outside. Playing "*Shaft*" in the stuffy band room was one thing; playing it while marching along in tight formation with forty other souls was big-time intimidating. Marching around in squads while playing an instrument calls for an athletic coordination arguably comparable to the game such a feat is designed to celebrate. Halfbacks would disagree with this, but I'd like to see you try to snap your knees and pivot on a yard line while playing from memory a flurry of sixteenth notes. Belly was more drill sergeant, finally, than band leader. He ran the band like a platoon. Girls had to pin their hair up under their shiny-billed caps. Guys would be cut from the band if their hair happened to reach their collars.

"*Shaft*" is brassy, a song for horns, and our squad was uncharacteristically integral. For weeks Belly was all over us in practice. He marched alongside, shouting his orders in a shrill bark, humiliating, embarrassing, mocking, making merciless fun of our sluggish stepping, our lack of snap, our weak bend of knee. He was hardest on me because he could be, given the tender racial climate. I bore the

"Now we were about to premiere, for an audience suspecting more anemic halftime show standards, the hottest jam of the Black Moses, Mr. Hot Buttered Soul himself. I envisioned the entire crowd, especially the grandstand, erupting in riotous ass-shake when we laid down that inimitable, high-hat cymbal-ticking introduction." Mr. Hot Buttered Soul, courtesy of http://www.isaachayes.com/.

brunt of Belly's ire for our missed pivots, our inevitable out-of-stepness. The others took note.

"Belly, man, he hate you," Cedrick said to me.

Butter: "Damn sure do."

Winnie: "What all'd you do to that fool make him act so ill at you?"

"I hate that sonofabitch right back," I said, ignoring Winnie's question, the answer to which would involve exposing all grades of racial animosity I gleaned from Belly's torment.

Across the field we marched, often until nine or ten on school nights in those weeks before Homecoming. Game week we marched until punch drunk. Butter lost some weight that week. All our uniforms drooped further toward the football field. Belly pushed us right up until the game.

Then halftime. The Dark Horses were getting trounced by Lakewood; they needed the shot of adrenaline only that bad mother SHAFT could provide. We took our places on the field. You could smell the nervousness, the sweat-weighted summer wool souring as we stood there, waiting.

But when the drum major lifted his baton, we missed the cue. Rather, half of us missed it and came in a few seconds late, so that the beginning, that signature rhythm-guitar chug translated to trumpets and tubas, baritones and trombones, echoed off the field house in a distracting, thunderous syncopation.

It got worse. The flutes were screechy, the clarinets sounded like scalded cats. Usually, while marching, it was difficult for us to actually hear the notes we were playing—we marched from memory, focused more on our feet than the song coming from our instruments—but that night, mid-deep in badass Shaft, half of us seemed to me marching to one song, the other half to a completely different tune. Then Butterball, our anchor, forgot to pivot, and we four clashed wildly with the stick girl flutists, as if we were out there playing ball, Butter a middle linebacker, the rest of us flanking tackles.

There was no way to come back. We just suffered through it. It's what you learn finally to do with failure and humiliation: lean right on into it. But I could not have realized that at the time. What was I expecting? Transcendence? Hendrix at Woodstock? Racial harmony? The comeuppance of Belly, who, humbled by our success, would change his militaristic manner and relax his conservative dress code? Did I really expect to ride right out of town on the soaring funky beat of a single watered-down Top-40 hit?

From the moment Butter sent the flutists stumbling, I pledged allegiance to Make Things Happen rather than sit around and wait. Marooned in mid-field shambles, I willed my hair to grow furiously toward my collar.

books

Matzoh Ball Gumbo

Culinary Tales of the Jewish South
By Marcie Cohen Ferris
University of North Carolina Press, 2005
327 pp. Cloth $29.95

Reviewed by **Dale Volberg Reed**, coauthor of
1001 Things Everyone Should Know About the South.

Growing up in East Tennessee I hardly knew any Jews, or hardly knew I knew any. Lacking the usual stereotypes, I didn't know, for example, that the owner of the nicest men's clothing store had both a name and an occupation that were most likely Jewish. When we spent a year in Jerusalem in 1973–74, I learned a bit about kashrut, which didn't strike me as at all odd, since I had grown up with Methodist dietary restrictions. "Thou shalt not drink" is less biblical and less poetic than the Jewish rules, but equally strict—and equally often ignored.

That same year Melville scholar Hennig Cohen visited Jerusalem, and I heard him describe, in his melting South Carolina accent, his family's Seder tradition of having the cook come out to the dining room and recite her version of F D R's "Stab in the Back" speech. Almost immediately thereafter I read Eli Evans's *The Provincials* (1973), and I realized that southern Jews are one of our most fascinating ethnic groups. Like many other groups, southern Jews became more self-conscious in the 1970s: the moribund Southern Jewish Historical Society was revived in 1976 and has flourished ever since, as has the topic of southern Jewry in both scholarly and popular literature. The many examples that come to mind include Louis Rubin's *My Father's People: A Family of Southern Jews*, Melissa Fay Greene's *The Temple Bombing*, Alfred Uhry's *Driving Miss Daisy*, and the beautiful and scholarly *A Portion of the People: Three Hundred Years of Southern Jewish Life*, edited by Theodore and Dale Rosengarten to accompany their art exhibition of the same name.

Recently, interest in foodways has gained academic respectability as a useful way to look at society and southern studies has continued to flourish, so it was almost inevitable that in 1999 the Southern Foodways Alliance was formed to combine the two. Take Jewish studies and southern studies, add study of southern foodways, throw in oral history, which everyone is doing these days, and you get *Matzoh Ball Gumbo*, the book Marcie Ferris was born to write.

Incidentally, I should state up front that I am a friend of Marcie Ferris's. I imagine that the editors of this journal couldn't find anyone interested in either southern Jews or southern food who is *not* a friend of Marcie's.

Marcie has been working on this project since she took her first bite of solid food, but I expect she began her first serious research when she realized Jews weren't supposed to eat at the Dixie Pig, in her hometown of Blytheville, Arkansas. Her background in museum work and public history, especially her time at the Museum of the Southern Jewish Experience, has given her the broad understanding of social history that is essential in any study of southern Jews. She has seen at first hand the effects of the social changes that have come with the South's urbanization: one of the museum's roles was to take care of the many Torahs belonging to defunct small-town southern congregations. (I have a cousin, the only adult Jew left in her town, who sees herself as personally responsible for the upkeep of the Jewish cemetery.)

Marcie's subtitle, "Culinary Tales of the Jewish South," reveals that this is a good southern book, based on stories rather than statistics. It's conversational, warm, and tasty. It may have begun life as a Ph.D. dissertation, but it almost never reveals its origin. It was probably the only charming dissertation her advisors had ever seen. I know, "charming dissertation" seems like an oxymoron, but I promise, it's not.

The book is divided into five main sections devoted to five distinct communities of southern Jews, in the lowcountry (Charleston and Savannah), Atlanta, New Orleans, the Mississippi Delta, and Memphis. Each section has history, anecdotes, interviews, and a few recipes, and in each we find a kaleidoscopic variety of ways to look at being southern through being Jewish, and vice-versa. In the lowcountry and New Orleans, the defining issue is usually shellfish (one Charlestonian says the three categories of food are not milk, meat, and pareve, but milk, meat, and shrimp; Temple Sinai in New Orleans holds an annual "seafood bingo" night), but in Memphis it's barbecue.

Speaking of barbecue, I have some bones to pick, not with the author, but with her publisher. No book is without errors, but this one has too many that shouldn't have made it through the editing process. They're individually too trivial to list here, but I expected more from a venerable and highly respected southern academic press.

Ignore them as best you can because this book is just plain fun, as well as being serious and thought-provoking. It's full of fascinating facts: Charleston had more Jews than New York in 1800 and was the birthplace of reform Judaism in America; Atlanta's branch of the National Council of Jewish Women offered classes in southern cooking to recent eastern European Jewish immigrants; Procter and Gamble's publicity slogan, "The Hebrew Race has been waiting 4,000 years for Crisco," resonated powerfully in a South fueled by lard. It's full of interesting ways to eat southern and still keep kosher, like flavoring black-eyed peas with kosher salami or cooking kosher turkeys in a Cajun deep-fryer. Most entertainingly, it's full of typically southern mental gymnastics designed to get around uncomfortable realities: Shabbat begins at sunset on Friday, but one synagogue moved its services to 6:00 PM so they would be over in time for the Friday night football game; a Charlestonian avoided oysters for Passover ("You can't eat oysters on Pesach, because there is no "r" in Pesach"); a joke features an orthodox man with an extra set of false teeth for barbecue.

Marcie obviously had fun finding the splendid illustrations. I love the photo of a birthday party in Asheville in 1931 featuring eight black nurses with their eight little charges, and the ad for White Swan Shortening with its Mammy figure saying, "Aint no Hog Fat in Dis Pie." And the ad, in Yiddish, for "Aunt Jemima's Latkes, with the Beloved Old Plantation Flavor" must be seen to be believed.

This is the sort of book that causes you to interrupt your spouse's work to read bits aloud. It will be at the top of my gift list for almost everyone next year, and it should certainly be on your bookshelf.

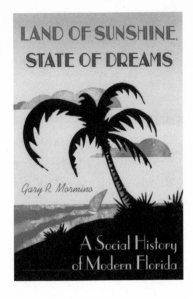

Land of Sunshine, Land of Dreams

A Social History of Modern Florida
By Gary R. Mormino
University Press of Florida, 2005
457 pp. Cloth, $34.95

Reviewed by **Stephen J. Whitfield**, professor
of American Studies at Brandeis University.

A glum paradox is embedded in the recent history of Florida. "I spent thirty years of my life trying to get people to move down there," the former mayor of Orlando has recalled. "And then they all did." In dreams begin responsibilities, which can lead to repercussions. The glad hand that for a century Florida residents have extended to tourists and to land developers, to senescent retirees and to spring-break hedonists has been so accepted that the consequences have been appalling: environmental degradation, traffic congestion, and the sort of sprawl that implies a kind of devotion to ugliness. The much touted attractions of the state—its sublime and tranquil beauty, its glistening beaches, its wish-you-were-here weather—became all too obvious; and a stunning growth in population has facilitated not only spectacular prosperity but also resulted in the staggering problems associated with uncontrolled growth. When Carl T. Langford, the Orlando mayor who played the role of booster a little too persuasively, decided to retire, he moved to North Carolina.

To the whole cluster of crises that Mach-2 modernization produces, Florida can be considered a first responder. At the dawn of the twentieth century, perhaps no southern state was sleepier; indeed until the end of the 1960s, even the Tallahassee legislature met only every other year—for sixty days. Before World War II, when Gary R. Mormino's account begins, no state seemed less relevant to the challenges that urbanization and industrialization were posing elsewhere. In 1940 no southern state had fewer residents. Before the end of the century, Florida had become the nation's fourth most populous state, and is coming on so fast on the outside that soon even New York will be outpaced. Only one Florida county was needed to decide the 2000 election, with consequences for the planet that have yet to be calibrated. Florida's latitudes do not correspond, however, with its attitudes; a smaller slice of its residents think of themselves as southern than any state that seceded from the union. Florida even became the first ex-Confederate state to harbor a majority of whites who were born outside the region.

Indeed the combustible, dynamic heterogeneity of Florida casts doubt on the meaning of regionalism — the organizing principle that has bewitched many an American historian and social scientist. Texas can at least be attached to the West. But if Florida does not belong to a region that includes, say, Alabama or Arkansas, where can this behemoth be inserted? And if Florida must therefore be subsumed into the South that was long preceded by the adjective "solid," how are essential features of Dixie's identity altered — and even rendered suspect? The jacket photo poses Mormino at a beach — a background that would have been incongruous in showcasing the books of W. J. Cash or C. Vann Woodward.

To trace the astonishing transformations of Florida since World War II requires an historian of uncommon skill; but Mormino, who is (inevitably) not a native, is up to the task. Based at the University of South Florida at St. Petersburg, he brings a breathless enthusiasm to his subject, which is illumined through vivid prose and impressively diligent research. Over four dozen of the state's local newspapers have been culled, in addition to more predictable national sources. The standard scholarly journal, the *Florida Historical Quarterly*, apparently failed to keep up with the tempo of change in the last half century and is barely cited, however. Mormino is serious about the scope of his subtitle: this is social history from which politics has been firmly excluded (although even he cannot ignore the vehement anti-Communism of south Florida's Cubans in affecting American foreign policy in the Caribbean). The text of *Land of Sunshine, State of Dreams* is sprinkled with a huge array of interesting data, adroitly deployed to back up the claims of demographic and economic cataclysm. But this book cannot be expected to earn the unalloyed endorsement of the Chamber of Commerce, because Mormino's chapters tend to be organized around the melancholy effects of rapacity; the Big Bang has meant a deterioration in the quality of life.

This book deserves a readership outside of modern Florida itself in part because Mormino is a marvelous storyteller. No incident better reveals the shift to a flamboyantly postindustrial Florida than the miscommunication that occurred early in the 1960s, when the controller of the duPont family fortune and of the St. Joe Land Company, Ed Ball, took a phone call from Walt Disney. Envisioning what would in 1971 become Walt Disney World, the California entrepreneur was very, very interested in buying up real estate. But Ball, who was the largest landowner in the state, demurred; and when Disney called back, he was subjected to the following brush-off: "We don't deal with carnival people."

Selected Poems

By James Applewhite
Duke University Press, 2005
184 pp. Paper $18.95

Reviewed by **Robert M. West**, assistant
professor of English at Mississippi State
University.

It's remarkable how often the national poetry establishment fails to celebrate the many fine southern poets writing today. Our poets win an oddly small number of major literary awards, and they appear in far too few anthologies of national scope. No informed person could seriously argue that contemporary southern poetry is on the whole inferior to contemporary northeastern or west coast poetry, but the national scene is dominated by poets from those regions. Even when southerners manage to break through to some form of national acknowledgment, the stalwart anthologists often hold the line. The new, third edition of the *Norton Anthology of Modern Poetry* expands that standard textbook to two volumes, but still finds no room for Bollingen Prize-winning Fred Chappell or Pulitzer Prize-winning Henry Taylor. And Maya Angelou and Miller Williams may have built reputations that won them commissions for Presidential Inaugural poems, but neither has ever appeared in the annual *Best American Poetry* series. The chief tastemakers of contemporary American poetry, Harold Bloom and Helen Vendler, clearly believe that American poetic talent is concentrated in the Northeast; when they do exalt contemporary southerners, those poets (chiefly Robert Penn Warren, A. R. Ammons, and Charles Wright) have typically either moved to the Northeast or established second homes there. For recent poets, southernness tends to be a handicap.

All of which makes it especially interesting that James Applewhite, unmistakably a southerner, has managed to win fame at the national level. Born and bred in eastern North Carolina, Applewhite attended Duke University; he began his career as an English professor at the University of North Carolina at Greensboro, and in 1972 he returned to Duke, where he teaches today. The poetry itself is as southern as the man, routinely engaging as it does with the region's culture and landscape. Despite his background in and persistent concern with the South, Applewhite has in recent years been lauded by "national" critics and poet-critics. For instance,

John Hollander included Applewhite's "Botanical Garden: The Coastal Plains" in *The Best American Poetry 1998*, and in *The Western Canon* Harold Bloom wagered that Applewhite's book *River Writing: An Eno Journal* would eventually be regarded as a canonical text. Of the three blurbs on the back of Applewhite's new *Selected Poems*, one is by fellow southerner Dave Smith, but the other two are by Bloom and New York School poet John Ashbery. Bloom writes that Applewhite "has individuated a logical and meditative voice all his own," and adds that he is one of only "a few living American poets who fuse so remarkably intellect and emotion"; Ashbery says that Applewhite writes "in language whose timeless gravity and sweetness are close to sublime" and deems the *Selected Poems* "an essential book." A poet must be doing something right to earn such recognition and praise.

And he is. For one thing, these poems demonstrate a genuine gift for figurative thinking and writing; often they provide extraordinary recastings of the extraordinary. Consider the talk of two tobacco farmers in "Some Words for Fall": Applewhite tells us, "The language they speak is things to eat." (Michael McFee borrowed this line for the title of his fine North Carolina poetry anthology.) Or the poet's response to an altar call in "A Forge of Words": "From the anvil of Christ, I receive my hammered name." Or the onset of evening in "Like a Body in the River": "The sepia light rusted toward oblivion." Some of the book's very best poems—such as "Water," "Jonquils," and "Collards"—are virtuosic exercises in trope-making, one metaphor or simile leading to the next from beginning to end. Ezra Pound's famous dictum, "Make it new," is one that Applewhite follows time and again, hallowing the everyday through his verbal transformations. As he explains in "Prayer for My Son," "any tree is a marvelous city."

Such metamorphosis is valuable in itself, for the way it helps us appreciate things and customs we've come to take for granted—but for Applewhite it also operates in the service of a powerful sociohistorical vision, one anguished over the past and the present, hardly daring to hope for a better future. For example, in "Tobacco Men," after recalling half a dozen field workers he once knew, Applewhite concludes the poem by addressing them:

> I search for your faces in relation
> To a tobacco stalk I can see,
> One fountain of up-rounding leaf.
> It looms, expanding, like an oak.
> Your faces form fruit where branches are forking.
> Like the slow-motion explosion of a thunderhead,
> It is sucking the horizon to a bruise.
> A cloud's high forehead wears ice.

To call such a passage surrealistic does it no justice; it's dazzlingly hallucinatory, but it's also clearly metaphorical. The tobacco men are as much a product of the land as the plant they cultivate, harvest, and cure; they may as well be part of the plant itself. Both human and vegetative, rooted to the soil, certainly not free, they play a largely unconscious role in a "slow-motion" but nevertheless terrible health crisis. The density of the figurative play here is remarkable: the expanding stalk in the vision is compared to a growing thunderhead, which in turn suggests both a giant puff of tobacco smoke *and* a coming catastrophe. And floating above it all? A cloud with a high and icy forehead, a hint of a merciless Almighty gazing down on all this folly.

Applewhite's perspective on white-black race relations is nearly as bleak as his perspective on tobacco. Indeed, like many white southern writers he seems haunted by the matter of race. In "My Grandfather's Funeral," moving from the church to the cemetery, he is "not prepared" for the sudden reappearance of the world, including "Negroes / In clothes the colors of the earth they plowed." In "Visit with Artina" he gives voice to an old woman with "cocoa skin" who used to work for his family: "Back when I worked for your folks," she says, "I felt burdened down, / Like everybody else was higher." In "Evening in Bath," one of his chief memories is of an elderly British woman who "hoped we'd not let / Blacks marry whites in the States." In "The Failure of Southern Representation," he complains of "Accents which deep in their vowels have / Never given up the slaves." The most complete statement on race relations comes late in the book, in "After *Winslow Homer's Images of Blacks.*" Pausing during a run, the poem's unnamed "he" (presumably the poet himself) has a vision of "brown Bit, . . . his mother for a time," along with other black women who are "moaning softly . . . the pain-song of everyday work, of hidden / selves, of roles worn habitually, to please even him, / when he was young." He also imagines he sees his parents, who

> are saying with their eyes and lips that it
> was hurt and humiliation they inherited, and allowed
> him to share in — a poor fare like collards boiled
> until vitamins were gone, like corn bread with flavoring
> of ashes[.]

He inherits the shame of the white South's defeat in war, but also the shame of its racism, of its failure to work out a true harmony between white and black southerners. Even the ground at his feet seems to testify to that continuing failure: he sees sand and brown pine needles, "irreducible colors / from his past, the pale and the brown together, / not mixing."

Randall Jarrell once suggested that even a great poet may write only a dozen poems of real distinction. Certainly any poet's work is uneven, and the most impressive poems are going to make up a fairly small percentage of his or her total oeuvre. Some of Applewhite's work, even in the *Selected Poems*, falls rather short of his best: the language of the early poems can be frustratingly imprecise, and his ear, sure in his usual free verse, is less so when he writes in rhyme. Sometimes a poem's rhetorical gesture can itself be awkward, as in "Grandfather Wordsworth," where he addresses his great predecessor three times as "William." (Imagine Wordsworth in "London, 1802" addressing Milton as "John.") Yet such slips matter little next to Applewhite's triumphs, poems such as "Tobacco Men," "Water," "Some Words for Fall," "Jonquils," "Collards," "How to Fix a Pig," "Prayer for My Son," "A Wilson County Farmer," "After *Winslow Homer's Images of Blacks*," "Botanical Garden: The Coastal Plains," the Wordsworthian "Autumnal Equinox," and a brilliant reflection on the papacy, "A Distant Father." In these portraits and meditations we see a poet who deserves acclaim not just across the South, but across the nation.

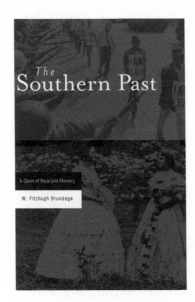

The Southern Past

A Clash of Race and Memory
By W. Fitzhugh Brundage
Harvard University Press, 2005
418 pp. Cloth $29.95

Reviewed by **John Bodnar**, Chancellor's
Professor and Chair of the history department,
Indiana University, Bloomington.

Fitzhugh Brundage's excellent book takes up the subject of public forms of remembering and commemoration in the South since the Civil War. He sees well that the region's collective memory was implicated in a wider political struggle for power and identity that would favor whites over blacks. The inevitable clash of remembering and forgetting that marks all public memory projects was not only driven here by matters of race but was a decidedly visible process where "an enduring white memory" and "black resistance to it" clashed frequently in public ceremonies, institutions, and politics. This was not the stuff of backroom deals. Thus, he offers insightful essays on the "robust ceremonial life" of African Americans and their efforts to preserve a history of the Civil War that featured emancipation, on the efforts to create in the 1920s a celebration called

Negro History Week, and on the rise of civil rights museums in the 1980s. Whites are seen fashioning a more nostalgic version of the past centered on the idea of the Old South and preserved in countless memorials, tourist sites, and state archives.

Brundage's account of these southern cultural wars extends the work of David Blight's *Race and Reunion: The Civil War in American Memory*, which also stressed the role of race in shaping the way Americans recalled the Civil War. In Blight's book white veterans in both the South and the North worked to craft a story of the war that was centered on the celebration of male valor in battle. Common valor allowed these men to foster a sense of reunion and national reconciliation—and forget that the war was also about equal rights for African Americans. For both Blight and Brundage, black commemorative activity worked to sustain the more democratic and egalitarian remembrance of the conflict. Brundage's story, however, pays little heed to the attractions of national unity and memory. His whites and African Americans appear locked in a conflict that seems essentially regional. African Americans continue in his book to evoke national traditions such as Independence Day in order to insist that they be included in the nation as equals. What better way to contest their marginalization in southern life? Had Brundage probed more deeply the impact of world wars on commemoration in the South in the twentieth century, I suspect he would have uncovered a continued discussion over the relationship between southerners of both races in the larger "imagined community" of America.

Race is such a powerful factor, however, that it certainly allows for an insightful look at the public debates over a southern past. Indeed, Brundage's account actually covers a wider array of memory sites and battles than Blight's. Thus, Brundage takes readers on original excursions into movements to organize state archives in the South and into projects to create tourist attractions focusing on the "colonial elegance" of Charleston that fostered a nostalgic view of the region largely devoid of the sordid reality of slavery. He makes a valuable contribution when he explains the importance of public schools and historically black colleges. Denied substantial influence in public institutions, these schools were among the few places left to African Americans where a few dedicated educators could actually promote the study of "Negro history" during a period of white supremacy.

At the end of the story we find progress toward the creation of a shared past, with African American history projects and civil rights museums emerging throughout the South after the 1960s. Generally this movement was contingent upon a greater realization of the region's misdeeds than its heroic achievements. But the pull of the heroic and the mythical is still evident in the defense of Confederate symbols and even in the "uplifting" stories of civil rights leaders. The vast debate over public memory in our times—arguments often centering on war, genocide, and racial violence—has made it clear that the desire to retreat to a mythical past freed of the countless tragedies of history and a sense of responsibility for them is powerful. Such impulses explain the reluctance of some nations to come to terms with their activities in past wars and the continuing power of romantic versions of national and group identity. Yet, if there is to be a collective memory—for a region or a nation—that promotes larger visions of human rights and tolerance, the modern scholarship on cultural memory, and this book, tell us that tales of tragedy, brutality, and loss must be retained. This will be a challenge for all, regardless of racial or national background.

....

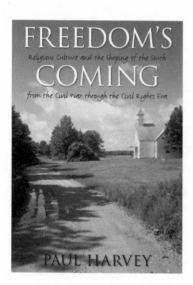

Freedom's Coming
Religious Culture and the Shaping
of the South from the Civil War
through the Civil Rights Era
By Paul Harvey
University of North Carolina Press, 2005
360 pp. Cloth $34.95

Reviewed by **Matt J. Zacharias Harper**, a Ph.D. candidate in history at the University of North Carolina at Chapel Hill who is currently researching African American Christianity in North Carolina.

If you think you understand how religion and race work in the South, then obviously no one has explained it to you properly. Lillian Smith tried to explain it in her 1949 *Killers of the Dream*: "We were taught . . . to love God, to love our white skin, and to believe in the sanctity of both." But it was more complicated than that, she admitted. "No wonder that God and Negroes and Jesus and sin and salvation are baled up together in southern children's minds and in many an old textile magnate's too." I suspect that quotes like these find their way into Paul Harvey's most recent book, *Freedom's Coming*, because he, too, recognizes the difficulty of making sense of how evangelicalism could mean so much to such different southerners as klansmen, populists, and civil rights activists.

Freedom's Coming is a broad, sweeping history of the South from Reconstruction to the 1990s. Harvey begins by noting the parallels between political and religious organizing after the Civil War and by discussing the different religious meanings southerners gave the War. He describes how the mainstream religious cultures of white supremacy and black independence left little room for white Unionists. Following other historians, Harvey presents both Reconstruction and redemption as religious movements, and he pays careful attention to the switch in white supremacist theology from paternalistic control in biracial churches to a justification of apartheid.

Freedom's Coming devotes considerable space to "thin but tough" groups of Christian dissenters who opened the South up for interracialism and undermined, if only in part, theological racism. The middle of the book is peopled by the likes of white liberals, Methodists, black Baptists turned NAACP organizers, the Disciples of Christ and the Southern Farmer's Alliance, Clarence Jordan and Koinonia Farm, Lucy R. Morgan and CIO labor movements, and Charles Jones and the Federation of Southern Churchmen. Harvey also investigates interracial spaces: places where black and white believers shared faith, ideas, and art. This Christian interracialism took place in music halls, Holiness-Pentecostal revivals, and over the radio. And although it was intermittent and often riddled with persistent beliefs in white superiority, it began to make fissures in the solid South. But what ultimately cracked it open was the mass movement of black southerners in the 1950s and 1960s. Evangelical piety, Harvey argues, was crucial to the movement's success, even if civil rights activists often expressed frustration that black churches and ministers were reluctant to get involved. For white churches, Harvey continues, the civil rights era was a time of "colossal moral failure," even though "there was considerable (if ultimately ineffectual) effort within white denominations to move beyond their history and legacy of theological racism."

In his final chapter, Harvey advances a provocative and compelling thesis. After the collapse of southern apartheid, conservative white Protestants abandoned and repented of theological racism. In its place, they placed increasing importance on what they deemed as God-given gender hierarchies. Advocating racial reconciliation and "wifely submission," the conservative leadership of the Southern Baptist Convention serves as the best example for Harvey's argument. Harvey fails to place this move in the context of Roman Catholics or nonsouthern conservative evangelicals, whose gender hierarchies are the subject of recent good sociological studies. Hardly a southern thing, patriarchy in American evangelicalism need not be so closely linked to the end of Jim Crow.

Harvey has done substantial primary research, but little of his story is new material. Rather, Harvey has found a way to string together ideas and examples from the best scholarly books on Reconstruction, Jim Crow, and the Civil Rights movement. Because *Freedom's Coming* so perfectly digests the best new works on the South, this is the place to play catch-up on southern religious scholarship. The footnotes and bibliography alone are worth the price of admission. His overarching argument—that southern evangelicals were not at ease in Zion, that even the most adamant white supremacist Christians felt tension about Jim Crow—makes room for us to see many Souths, including the South that Lillian Smith lamented and the South that she worked to create. Harvey's interpretive framework deserves praise because it can make sense of such diverse and divergent material, weds practice to theology, and rightfully places southern evangelical women at the center of the story. The religious cultures of the South are too important and too unwieldy to be exhausted by one book, but if you're looking for a place to start, there isn't a better place than *Freedom's Coming*.

About the Contributors

Michael Cohen is Chancellor's Post-doctoral Fellow in the history department at the University of California at Berkeley. He is working on a book entitled *The Conspiracy of Capital*.

Larry J. Griffin is coeditor of *Southern Cultures* and the John Shelton Reed Distinguished Professor of Sociology and professor of history at the University of North Carolina at Chapel Hill. He is now studying southern whites' memories of the Jim Crow and Civil Rights eras in the South and exploring whether they suggest personal or collective responsibility, shame, and guilt.

Edward John Harcourt writes about the social and cultural history of the Civil War Era and is author of "The Whipping of Richard Moore: Reading Emotion in Reconstruction America" (*Journal of Social History* 36 [Winter 2002]) and "Who Were the Pale Faces?: New Perspectives on the Tennessee Ku Klux" (*Civil War History* 51 [March 2005]).

Trudier Harris is J. Carlyle Sitterson Professor of English at the University of North Carolina at Chapel Hill. She has published widely and lectured across the country and the world in her specialty areas of African American literature and folklore. Her books include *From Mammies to Militants: Domestics in Black American Literature*, *The Power of the Porch: The Storyteller's Craft in Zora Neale Hurston, Gloria Naylor, and Randall Kenan*, and a memoir, *Summer Snow: Reflections from a Black Daughter of the South*.

Michael Parker is the prize-winning author of six books of fiction. His stories also have appeared in many magazines, including *Five Points*, *Shenandoah*, *Carolina Quarterly*, *The Oxford American*, and *The Georgia Review*, and have been widely anthologized. In 2004 he was awarded fiction fellowships from the North Carolina Arts Council and the National Endowment for the Arts. He is a professor in the MFA writing program at the University of North Carolina at Greensboro, where he teaches courses in creative writing and literature.

John Sledge is an architectural historian with the Mobile Historic Development Commission and books editor for the *Mobile Register*. **Sheila Hagler** is a freelance photographer who lives in Grand Bay, Alabama. Before working together on *An Ornament to the City: Old Mobile Ironwork*, from which their *Southern Cultures* photo essay is drawn, Sledge and Hagler collaborated on *Cities of Silence*, an illustrated study of Mobile's historic cemeteries.

The First Annual *Southern Cultures* Music Issue will be out soon—and it features a free CD.

Hear B. B. King musing about the blues while he strums Lucille, plus classic cuts from the Red Clay Ramblers and many *rare* Southern tracks.

Subscribe or renew today, and your new subscription will even include next year's music issue, too—plus a FREE BONUS ISSUE!

- -

Yes, sign me up for my music issues, included in my subscription ___ for 1 year ($28), ___ for 2 years ($49), or ___ for 3 years ($69), *and* send my BONUS ISSUE, too.

My check or money order, made payable to *Southern Cultures*, is enclosed with this form   OR   please charge my
___ VISA or ___ my MASTERCARD [check one].

Signature _____ phone _____
Card number_____ Exp. date _____
Name and address _____
_____ Zip code _____

MAIL to: CB# 9127, UNC-CH, Chapel Hill, NC 27599
CALL: (919) 966-3561, extension 256   FAX: 1-800-272-6817
EMAIL: uncpress_journals@unc.edu
ORDER ON-LINE: www. SouthernCultures.org
(For on-line orders, type "Bonus Issue" under *Comments*.)

- -

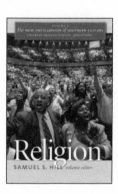
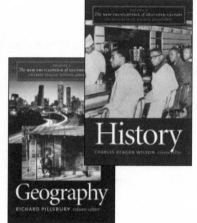
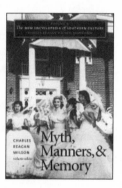

THE ART OF A GOOD READ

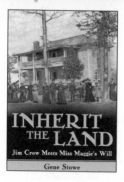

Inherit the Land
Jim Crow Meets
Miss Maggie's Will
By Gene Stowe
Illustrations by Carl A. Sergio
The history of a legal fight
in which an all-white jury
awarded African Americans a
North Carolina estate
$35 hardback

Mayor Crump
Don't Like It
Machine Politics in
Memphis
By G. Wayne Dowdy
A biography of the politician
who forged one of the first
biracial Democratic coalitions
in the 1930s South
$38 hardback

Rednecks, Redeemers,
and Race
Mississippi after
Reconstruction, 1877–1917
By Stephen Cresswell
A history of the paradoxi-
cal time when the state's
technology advanced and race
relations deteriorated
$45 hardback

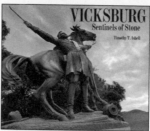

Vicksburg
Sentinels of Stone
By Timothy T. Isbell
"Tim Isbell has captured the
artful essence and humanity of
the monuments....The long,
complex Vicksburg campaign
has been relatively overlooked
by historians and the American people, and Isbell's work
will surely help to rectify that
unjust neglect." —Michael B.
Ballard, Civil War historian
and author of *Vicksburg:The
Campaign That Opened the
Mississippi*
$40 hardback

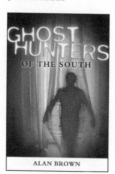

Ghost Hunters
of the South
By Alan Brown
From across the South,
profiles of irrepressible
investigators of the
paranormal
**$50 unjacketed hardback,
$20 paperback**

Dunlap
By William Dunlap
Essay by J. Richard Gruber
Foreword by Julia Reed
The first full-length book
heralding this world-renowned
artist's achievements over the
last thirty years
$45 hardback, $200 limited edition

Just Above the Water
Florida Folk Art
*By Kristin G. Congdon
and Tina Bucuvalas*
Foreword by Michael Owen Jones
An extensive study of the Sunshine State's folk art legacy and
the many cultures it represents
$65 hardback

Lost Plantation
The Rise and Fall of
Seven Oaks
By Marc R. Matrana
The story of a Louisiana
mansion, a planter's empire,
and a preservation battle lost
to bulldozers
$20 paperback

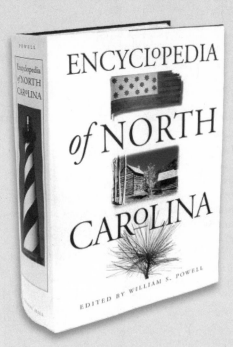

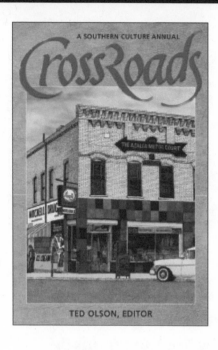

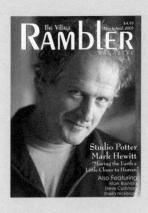
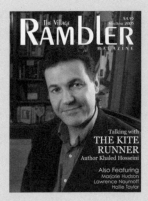

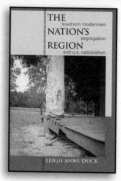

Mockingbird Song
Ecological Landscapes of the South

JACK TEMPLE KIRBY

With the intimacy and enthusiasm of a storyteller, Kirby explores the South's peoples and their landscapes.

"Moves in the most sure-footed way across a variety of themes, ranging from Bartram and alligators to parakeets and apple orchards.... A model for examinations of other regions."—John R. Stilgoe, author of *Landscape and Images*
384 pp., 29 illus., 5 maps $29.95 cloth

Walker Percy Remembered
A Portrait in the Words of Those Who Knew Him

DAVID HORACE HARWELL

"The reminiscences of a diverse group of Percy's neighbors, close friends, and kinspeople.... [provide] sharp insight and telling anecdotes [that reveal] why Percy was so beloved by those who knew him well.... A remarkable, poignant collection."—Bertram Wyatt-Brown, author of *The House of Percy*
200 pp. $24.95 cloth
Alternate Selection of the Readers' Subscription

Little Zion
A Church Baptized by Fire

SHELLY O'FORAN

"Movingly tells 'the half that has never been told,' effectively documenting the life, significance, and impact of a small rural antebellum church from the perspective of the African American church members."—Daryl Cumber Dance, author of *Shuckin' and Jivin'*
304 pp., 24 illus. $49.95 cloth / $19.95 paper

The Inner Islands
A Carolinian's Sound Country Chronicle

BLAND SIMPSON
Photography by Ann Cary Simpson

Blending history, oral history, autobiography, and travel narrative, Bland Simpson explores the geography and biodiversity of the islands that lie in eastern North Carolina's sounds, rivers, and swamps.
264 pp., 54 illus. $34.95 cloth

Super-Scenic Motorway
A Blue Ridge Parkway History

ANNE MITCHELL WHISNANT

Mining the historical archives, Anne Whisnant uncovers the twists and turns in the history of the seventy-year development of the beloved roadway.
480 pp., 40 illus., 8 maps $34.95 cloth

Sea Change at Annapolis

The United States Naval Academy, 1949–2000

H. MICHAEL GELFAND

Foreword by Senator John McCain

"Gelfand's interaction with midshipmen and in-depth interviews with many distinguished graduates and leaders help shape a lasting impression of an institution that depends on tradition and the ability to change to meet the requirements of the society it serves."—Bud Edney, Admiral USN (Ret.)

384 pp. $34.95 cloth

Sexuality, Politics, and Social Control in Virginia, 1920–1945

PIPPA HOLLOWAY

"An important contribution to our understanding of the politics of sexuality, social reform, and state formation in the mid-20th-century American South."—J. Douglas Smith, author of *Managing White Supremacy*

296 pp. $59.95 cloth / $19.95 paper

Pauli Murray and Caroline Ware

Forty Years of Letters in Black and White

ANNE FIROR SCOTT, EDITOR

"This intriguing collection of letters, edited by one of our most distinguished American historians, follows the evolving relationship between two very unlikely 'sisters' whose friendship doesn't quite fit any mold we might cast to surround it."—Barbara Ransby, author of *Ella Baker and the Black Freedom Movement*

Gender and American Culture

216 pp. $24.95 cloth

★ NEW IN PAPERBACK

Blood and Irony

Southern White Women's Narratives of the Civil War, 1861–1937

SARAH E. GARDNER

"As enlightening as it is enjoyable to read, [Gardner's] assessment of the popular myths and painful truths . . . gives to women their rightful place and influence in the interpretation of the Civil War and . . . a fresh perspective and better understanding of our nation's bloodiest conflict."—*Tennessee Advocate*

352 pp. $19.95 paper

John Tyler, the Accidental President

EDWARD P. CRAPOL

"Poignantly portrays the tragic irony of John Tyler's legacy to America. . . . Siding against the nation he once led, Tyler died in the midst of a war that gave the nation a new birth of freedom by destroying the social order that Tyler had championed."
—James M. McPherson, Princeton University

328 pp. $37.50 cloth

Southern **cultures**

For fastest service, please call [919] 966-3561, ext. 256, Monday–Friday between 8:00 a.m. and 3:00 p.m. EST with credit card information or fax your order to [800] 272-6817. You can also send e-mail to uncpress_journals@unc.edu.

INDIVIDUAL *subscription request*

Please enter my subscription to *Southern Cultures* at the rate of $28 for four quarterly issues. [Add $12 for postage outside the US.] *This price is good until December 31, 2006.*

☐ My check or money order, payable to THE UNIVERSITY OF NORTH CAROLINA PRESS, is enclosed in an envelope with this card.

☐ Please charge my Visa or MasterCard [circle one].

CARD NUMBER _____ EXP. DATE _____

SIGNATURE _____ DAYTIME PHONE _____

NAME _____

ADDRESS _____ ZIP CODE _____

Southern **cultures**

For fastest service, please call [919] 966-3561, ext. 256, Monday–Friday between 8:00 a.m. and 3:00 p.m. EST with credit card information or fax your order to [800] 272-6817. You can also send e-mail to uncpress_journals@unc.edu.

INSTITUTION *subscription request*

Please enter my subscription to *Southern Cultures* at the rate of $50 for four quarterly issues. [Add $12 for postage outside the US.] *This price is good until December 31, 2006.*

☐ My check or money order, payable to THE UNIVERSITY OF NORTH CAROLINA PRESS, is enclosed in an envelope with this card.

☐ Please charge my Visa or MasterCard [circle one].

CARD NUMBER _____ EXP. DATE _____

SIGNATURE _____ DAYTIME PHONE _____

NAME _____

ADDRESS _____ ZIP CODE _____

BUSINESS REPLY MAIL
FIRST-CLASS MAIL   PERMIT NO. 509   CHAPEL HILL, NC

POSTAGE WILL BE PAID BY ADDRESSEE

THE UNIVERSITY OF NORTH CAROLINA PRESS
JOURNALS FULFILLMENT
116 S BOUNDARY STREET
CHAPEL HILL, NC 27514-9943

NO POSTAGE
NECESSARY
IF MAILED
IN THE
UNITED STATES